Ninja Foodi Grill Cookbook #2021

The 365-day quick, delicious and affordable recipes for indoor grilling and air frying. Enjoy meals with your Ninja Foodi Grill.

ELIZABETH A. HARRIS

© Copyright 2020 - All rights reserved.

The content contained within this book may not be reproduced, duplicated or transmitted without direct written permission from the author or the publisher.

Under no circumstances will any blame or legal responsibility be held against the publisher, or author, for any damages, reparation, or monetary loss due to the information contained within this book. Either directly or indirectly.

Legal Notice:

This book is copyright protected. This book is only for personal use. You cannot amend, distribute, sell, use, quote or paraphrase any part, or the content within this book, without the consent of the author or publisher.

Disclaimer Notice:

Please note the information contained within this document is for educational and entertainment purposes only. All effort has been executed to present accurate, up to date, and reliable, complete information. No warranties of any kind are declared or implied. Readers acknowledge that the author is not engaging in the rendering of legal, financial, medical or professional advice. The content within this book has been derived from various sources. Please consult a licensed professional before attempting any techniques outlined in this book.

By reading this document, the reader agrees that under no circumstances is the author responsible for any losses, direct or indirect, which are incurred as a result of the use of information contained within this document, including, but not limited to, — errors, omissions, or inaccuracies.

BREAKFAST RECIPES	8
1. Cinnamon Buttered Toasts	9
2. Cheddar Mustard Toasts	9
3. Cinnamon French Toasts	10
4. Savory French Toasts	10
5. Eggs in Avocado Halves	11
6. Scallion & Jalapeño Soufflé	11
7. Baked Cheesy Eggs	12
8. Turkey & Spinach Bites	12
9. Bacon & Bread Cups	13
10. Spinach & Egg Bites	13
11. Bacon & Egg Cups	14
12. Cheese Omelet	15
13. Cheddar & Cream Omelet	15
14. Mushroom & Pepperoncini Omelet	16
15. Zucchini Omelet	16
16. Chicken Omelet	17
17. Pepperoni Omelet	17
18. Sausage & Bacon Omelet	18
19. Tofu Omelet	18
20. Sausage & Scallion Frittata	19
21. Pancetta & Spinach Frittata	19
22. Trout Frittata	20
23. Spinach & Tomato Frittata	20
24. Bacon & Mushroom Frittata	22
25. Mini Tomato Quiches	22
POULTRY RECIPES	23
26. Spiced Cornish Hen	24
27. Herbed Cornish Hen	25
28. Spicy Whole Chicken	26
29. Herbed Whole Chicken	27
30. Lemony Whole Chicken	28
31. Whole Chicken with Potatoes	29
32. Crispy Roasted Chicken	30
33. Spicy Chicken Legs	31
34. Crispy Chicken Legs	32
35. Sweet & Spicy Chicken Drumsticks	33
36. Glazed Chicken Drumsticks	34
37. Rosemary Chicken Thighs	35
38. Lemony Chicken Thighs	35
39. Marinated Chicken Thighs	36
40. Spiced Chicken Breasts	37
BEEF, PORK AND LAMB RECIPES	38
41. Simple Filet Mignon	39
42. Seasoned Filet Mignon	39
43. Seasoned Flank Steak	40
44. Sweet & Sour Flank Steak	41
45. Crispy Sirloin Steaks	42
46. Buttered Striploin Steak	42
47. Vinegar London Broil Steak	43
48. Herbed Beef Roast	44
49. Seasoned Beef Roast	44
50. Simple Beef Sirloin Roast	45
51. Glazed Pork Ribs	45
52. Simple Pork Loin	46
53. Basil Pork Loin	46
54. Glazed Pork Shoulder	47
55. Seasoned Pork Shoulder	48
56. Stuffed Pork Roll	49
57. Glazed Pork Tenderloin	50
58. Bacon-Wrapped Pork Tenderloin	51
59. Pork Loin with Potatoes	52
60. Pork Taco Casserole	53
61. Sausage Casserole	54
62. Glazed Ham	55
63. Marinated Lamb Chops	56

#	Title	Page
64.	Lamb Chops with Veggies	57
65.	Herbed Rack of Lamb	58
66.	Almond Crusted Rack of Lamb	59
67.	Pesto Rack of Lamb	60
68.	Parmesan Crusted Rack of Lamb	61
69.	Garlicky Lamb Steaks	62
70.	Lamb Rump with Carrots	63
71.	Glazed Leg of Lamb	64
72.	Garlicky Lamb Roast	65
73.	Lamb Meatloaf	66
74.	Lamb Stuffed Bell Peppers	67
75.	Spicy Lamb Burgers	68

FISH & SEAFOOD RECIPES 69

#	Title	Page
76.	Simple Salmon	70
77.	Buttered Salmon	70
78.	Zesty Salmon	71
79.	Cajun Salmon	71
80.	Teriyaki Salmon	72
81.	Buttered Halibut	72
82.	Sweet & Sour Salmon	73
83.	Glazed Haddock	74
84.	Simple Cod	75
85.	Crusted Sole	75
86.	Cod & Veggie Parcel	76
87.	Spicy Catfish	77
88.	Ranch Tilapia	78
89.	Lemony Shrimp	78
90.	Shrimp Scampi	79
91.	Shrimp Kabobs	80
92.	Thyme Scallops	81
93.	Scallops in Capers Sauce	81
94.	Scallops with Spinach	82
95.	Seafood Pasta	83

VEGETARIAN AND VEGAN RECIPES 84

#	Title	Page
96.	Veggie Ratatouille	85
97.	Nutty Acorn Squash	86
98.	Vegetarian Stuffed Bell Peppers	87
99.	Stuffed Pumpkin	88
100.	Vegetarian Loaf	89
101.	Beans & Veggie Burgers	90
102.	Tofu with Orange Sauce	91
103.	Mac n' Cheese	92

SIDE DISHES RECIPES 93

#	Title	Page
104.	Stuffed Tomatoes	94
105.	Pesto Tomatoes	95
106.	Cheesy Spinach	96
107.	Herbed Mushrooms	97
108.	Cheesy Mushrooms	98
109.	Glazed Carrots	98
110.	Lemony Green Beans	99
111.	Vinegar Brussels Sprout	99
112.	Seasoned Zucchini	100
113.	Parmesan Asparagus	100
114.	Stuffed Potatoes	101
115.	Jacket Potatoes	102
116.	Spicy Potatoes	103
117.	Herbed Bell Peppers	104
118.	Marinated Tofu	104

APPETIZER & SNACK RECIPES 105

#	Title	Page
119.	Buffalo Chicken Wings	106
120.	BBQ Chicken Wings	107
121.	Crispy Prawns	107
122.	Crispy Shrimp	108
123.	Bread Rolls	109
124.	Beef Taquitos	110
125.	Mixed Veggie Bites	111
126.	Feta Tater Tots	112
127.	Roasted Cashews	112

128.	Tortilla Chips	113
129.	Apple Chips	113
130.	Spinach Chips	114
131.	French Fries	114
132.	Zucchini Fries	115
133.	Mozzarella Sticks	116
134.	Chicken Nuggets	117
135.	Bacon Croquettes	118
136.	Potato Croquettes	119
137.	Broccoli Bites	120
138.	Cauliflower Poppers	121
139.	Spinach Dip	122
140.	Onion Dip	123

DESSERT RECIPES 124

141.	Lava Cake	125
142.	Butter Cake	126
143.	Chocolate Brownie Cake	127
144.	Mini Cheesecakes	128
145.	Vanilla Cheesecake	129
146.	Pumpkin Pie	130
147.	Pecan Pie	131
148.	Plum Crisps	132
149.	Cherry Clafoutis	133
150.	Lemon Mousse	134
151.	Apple Bread Pudding	135
152.	Chocolate Pudding	136

BREAKFAST RECIPES

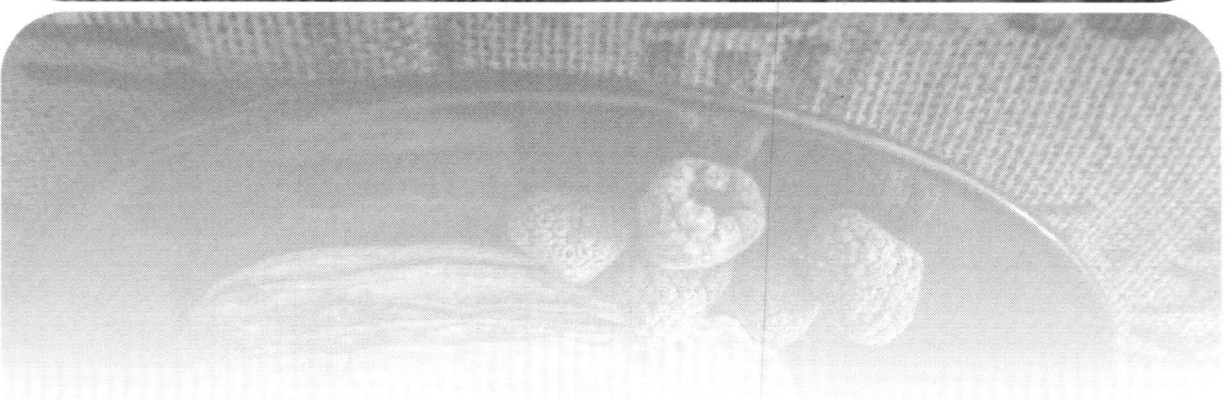

1. Cinnamon Buttered Toasts

⏱ Prep Time 10 m | ⏱ Cooking Time 5 m | 3 Servings

Ingredients:

- ¼ cup sugar
- ¾ teaspoon ground cinnamon
- ¾ teaspoon vanilla extract
- 1/8 teaspoons freshly ground black pepper
- ¼ cup salted butter, softened
- 6 whole-wheat bread slices

Instructions:

1. In a bowl, add the sugar, vanilla, cinnamon, black pepper and butter and mix until smooth.
2. Spread the butter mixture over each bread slice evenly.
3. Arrange the "Crisper Basket" in the pot of Ninja Foodi Grill.
4. Close the Ninja Foodi Grill with lid and select "Air Crisp".
5. Set the temperature to 400 degrees F to preheat.
6. Press "Start/Stop" to begin preheating.
7. When the display shows "Add Food" open the lid and place the bread slices into the "Crisper Basket".
8. Close the Ninja Foodi Grill with lid and set the time for 5 minutes.
9. Press "Start/Stop" to begin cooking.
10. When the cooking time is completed, press "Start/Stop" to stop cooking and open the lid.
11. Transfer the bread slices onto serving plates.
12. Cut each bread slice in half diagonally and serve.

Nutritional Information per Serving:

Calories: 341 | Fat: 17.2g | Saturated Fat: 10.1g | Carbohydrates: 40.5g | Sugar: 19.9g | Protein: 7.4g

2. Cheddar Mustard Toasts

⏱ Prep Time 10 m | ⏱ Cooking Time 10 m | 2 Servings

Ingredients:

- 4 bread slices
- 2 tablespoons cheddar cheese, shredded
- 2 eggs, whites and yolks, separated
- 1 tablespoon mustard
- 1 tablespoon paprika

Instructions:

1. In a clean glass bowl, add the egg whites and beat until they form soft peaks.
2. In another bowl, mix together the cheese, egg yolks, mustard, and paprika.
3. Gently fold in the egg whites.
4. Spread the mustard mixture over the toasted bread slices.
5. Arrange the greased "Crisper Basket" in the pot of Ninja Foodi Grill.
6. Close the Ninja Foodi Grill with lid and select "Air Crisp".
7. Set the temperature to 355 degrees F to preheat.
8. Press "Start/Stop" to begin preheating.
9. When the display shows "Add Food" open the lid and place the bread slices into the "Crisper Basket".
10. Close the Ninja Foodi Grill with lid and set the time for 10 minutes.
11. Press "Start/Stop" to begin cooking.
12. When the cooking time is completed, press "Start/Stop" to stop cooking and open the lid.
13. Transfer the bread slices onto serving plates.
14. Cut each bread slice in half diagonally and serve.

Nutritional Information per Serving:

Calories: 175 | Fat: 9.4g | Saturated Fat: 3.1g | Carbohydrates: 13.4g | Sugar: 1.9g | Protein: 10.6g

3. Cinnamon French Toasts

⏰ Prep Time 5 m | ⏰ Cooking Time 10 m | 2 Servings

Ingredients:

- 2 eggs
- ¼ cup whole milk
- 3 tablespoons Sugar:
- 2 teaspoons olive oil
- 1/8 teaspoon vanilla extract
- 1/8 teaspoon ground cinnamon
- 4 bread slices

Instructions:

1. In a large bowl, mix together all the ingredients except for bread slices.
2. Coat the bread slices with egg mixture evenly.
3. Arrange the lightly greased "Crisper Basket" in the pot of Ninja Foodi Grill.
4. Close the Ninja Foodi Grill with lid and select "Air Crisp".
5. Set the temperature to 390 degrees F to preheat.
6. Press "Start/Stop" to begin preheating.
7. When the display shows "Add Food" open the lid and place the bread slices into the "Crisper Basket".
8. Close the Ninja Foodi Grill with lid and set the time for 5 minutes.
9. Press "Start/Stop" to begin cooking.
10. Flip the bread slices once halfway through.
11. When the cooking time is completed, press "Start/Stop" to stop cooking and open the lid.
12. Transfer the bread slices onto serving plates.
13. Cut each bread slice in half diagonally and serve.

Nutritional Information per Serving:

Calories: 238 | Fat: 10.6g | Saturated Fat: 2.7g | Carbohydrates: 20.8g | Sugar: 0.9g | Protein: 7.9g

4. Savory French Toasts

⏰ Prep Time 5 m | ⏰ Cooking Time 10 m | 2 Servings

Ingredients:

- ¼ cup chickpea flour
- 3 tablespoons onion, finely chopped
- 2 teaspoons green chili, seeded and finely chopped
- ½ teaspoon red chili powder
- ¼ teaspoon ground turmeric
- ¼ teaspoon ground cumin
- Salt, to taste
- Water, as needed
- 4 bread slices

Instructions:

1. In a large bowl, add all the ingredients except for bread slices and mix until a thick mixture forms.
2. With a spoon, spread the mixture over both sides of each bread slice.
3. Arrange the bread slices into the lightly greased the baking pan.
4. Arrange the "Crisper Basket" in the pot of Ninja Foodi Grill.
5. Close the Ninja Foodi Grill with lid and select "Air Crisp".
6. Set the temperature to 390 degrees F to preheat.
7. Press "Start/Stop" to begin preheating.
8. When the display shows "Add Food" open the lid and place the baking pan into the "Crisper Basket".
9. Close the Ninja Foodi Grill with lid and set the time for 5 minutes.
10. Press "Start/Stop" to begin cooking.
11. Flip the bread slices once halfway through.
12. When the cooking time is completed, press "Start/Stop" to stop cooking and open the lid.
13. Transfer the bread slices onto serving plates.
14. Cut each bread slice in half diagonally and serve.

Nutritional Information per Serving:

Calories: 151 | Fat: 2.3g | Saturated Fat: 0.3g | Carbohydrates: 26.7g | Sugar: 4.3g | Protein: 6.5g

5. Eggs in Avocado Halves

⏰ Prep Time 10 m | ⏰ Cooking Time 10 m | 2 Servings

Ingredients:

- 1 avocado, halved and pitted
- 2 large eggs
- Salt and freshly ground black pepper, to taste
- 2 cooked bacon slices, crumbled

Instructions:

1. Carefully scoop out about 2 teaspoons of flesh from each avocado half.
2. Crack 1 egg in each avocado half and sprinkle with salt and black pepper.
3. Arrange the "Crisper Basket" in the pot of Ninja Foodi Grill.
4. Close the Ninja Foodi Grill with lid and select "Roast".
5. Set the temperature to 375 degrees F to preheat.
6. Press "Start/Stop" to begin preheating.
7. When the display shows "Add Food" open the lid and place the avocado halves into the "Crisper Basket".
8. Close the Ninja Foodi Grill with lid and set the time for 10 minutes.
9. Press "Start/Stop" to begin cooking.
10. When the cooking time is completed, press "Start/Stop" to stop cooking and open the lid.
11. Transfer the avocado halves onto serving plates.
12. Top each avocado half with bacon pieces and serve.

Nutritional Information per Serving:

Calories: 300 | Fat: 26.6g | Saturated Fat: 6.4g | Carbohydrates: 9g | Sugar: 0.9g | Protein: 9.7g

6. Scallion & Jalapeño Soufflé

⏰ Prep Time 8 m | ⏰ Cooking Time 10 m | 2 Servings

Ingredients:

- 2 tablespoons light cream
- 2 large eggs
- 1 tablespoon fresh scallion, chopped
- 1 jalapeño pepper, chopped
- Salt, to taste

Instructions:

1. Grease 2 soufflé dishes.
2. In a bowl, add all ingredients and beat until well combined.
3. Divide the mixture into the prepared soufflé dishes evenly.
4. Arrange the "Crisper Basket" in the pot of Ninja Foodi Grill.
5. Close the Ninja Foodi Grill with lid and select "Air Crisp".
6. Set the temperature to 390 degrees F to preheat.
7. Press "Start/Stop" to begin preheating.
8. When the display shows "Add Food" open the lid and place the soufflé dishes into the "Crisper Basket".
9. Close the Ninja Foodi Grill with lid and set the time for 8 minutes.
10. Press "Start/Stop" to begin cooking.
11. When the cooking time is completed, press "Start/Stop" to stop cooking and open the lid.
12. Serve hot.

Nutritional Information per Serving:

Calories: 82 | Fat: 5.7g | Saturated Fat: 2g | Carbohydrates: 1.3g | Sugar: 0.9g | Protein: 6.5g

7. Baked Cheesy Eggs

⏰ Prep Time 12 m | ⏰ Cooking Time 10 m | 4 Servings

Ingredients:

- 1 cup marinara sauce, divided
- 1 tablespoon capers, drained and divided
- 8 eggs
- ¼ cup whipping cream, divided
- ¼ cup parmesan cheese, shredded and divided
- Salt and freshly ground black pepper, to taste

Instructions:

1. Grease 4 ramekins.
2. Divide the marinara sauce in the bottom of each prepared ramekin evenly and top with capers.
3. Carefully crack 2 eggs over marinara sauce into each ramekin and top with cream, followed by the Parmesan cheese.
4. Sprinkle each ramekin with salt and black pepper.
5. Arrange the "Crisper Basket" in the pot of Ninja Foodi Grill.
6. Close the Ninja Foodi Grill with lid and select "Bake".
7. Set the temperature to 400 degrees F to preheat.
8. Press "Start/Stop" to begin preheating.
9. When the display shows "Add Food" open the lid and place the ramekins into the "Crisper Basket".
10. Close the Ninja Foodi Grill with lid and set the time for 12 minutes.
11. Press "Start/Stop" to begin cooking.
12. When the cooking time is completed, press "Start/Stop" to stop cooking and open the lid.
13. Serve warm.

Nutritional Information per Serving:

Calories: 223 | Fat: 14.1g | Saturated Fat: 5.5g | Carbohydrates: 9.8g | Sugar: 6.2g | Protein: 14.3g

8. Turkey & Spinach Bites

⏰ Prep Time 23 m | ⏰ Cooking Time 10 m | 4 Servings

Ingredients:

- 1 tablespoon unsalted butter
- 1 pound fresh baby spinach
- 4 eggs
- 7 ounces cooked turkey, chopped
- 4 teaspoons unsweetened almond milk
- Salt and freshly ground black pepper, to taste

Instructions:

1. In a frying pan, melt the butter over medium heat and cook the spinach for about 2-3 minutes or until just wilted.
2. Remove from the heat and drain the liquid completely.
3. Transfer the spinach into a bowl and set aside to cool slightly.
4. Divide the spinach into 4 greased ramekins, followed by the turkey.
5. Crack 1 egg into each ramekin and drizzle with almond milk.
6. Sprinkle with salt and black pepper.
7. Arrange the "Crisper Basket" in the pot of Ninja Foodi Grill.
8. Close the Ninja Foodi Grill with lid and select "Air Crisp".
9. Set the temperature to 355 degrees F to preheat.
10. Press "Start/Stop" to begin preheating.
11. When the display shows "Add Food" open the lid and place the ramekins into the "Crisper Basket".
12. Close the Ninja Foodi Grill with lid and set the time for 20 minutes.
13. Press "Start/Stop" to begin cooking.
14. When cooking time is completed, press "Start/Stop" to stop cooking and open the lid.
15. Serve hot.

Nutritional Information per Serving:

Calories: 200 | Fat: 10.2g | Saturated Fat: 4.1g | Carbohydrates: 4.5g | Sugar: 0.8g | Protein: 23.4g

9. Bacon & Bread Cups

⏰ Prep Time 10 m | ⏰ Cooking Time 10 m | 2 Servings

Ingredients:

- 2 bread slices
- 1 bacon slice, chopped
- 4 tomato slices
- 1 tablespoon mozzarella cheese, shredded
- 2 eggs
- 1/8 teaspoon maple syrup
- 1/8 teaspoon balsamic vinegar
- ¼ teaspoon fresh parsley, chopped
- Salt and freshly ground black pepper, to taste
- 2 tablespoons mayonnaise

Instructions:

1. Lightly grease 2 ramekins.
2. Line each prepared ramekin with 1 bread slice.
3. Divide the bacon and tomato slices over the bread slice in each ramekin.
4. Top with the cheese evenly.
5. Crack 1 egg in each ramekin over cheese.
6. Drizzle with maple syrup and vinegar and then sprinkle with parsley, salt and black pepper.
7. Arrange the "Crisper Basket" in the pot of Ninja Foodi Grill.
8. Close the Ninja Foodi Grill with lid and select "Air Crisp".
9. Set the temperature to 320 degrees F to preheat.
10. Press "Start/Stop" to begin preheating.
11. When the display shows "Add Food" open the lid and place the ramekins into the "Crisper Basket".
12. Close the Ninja Foodi Grill with lid and set the time for 10 minutes.
13. Press "Start/Stop" to begin cooking.
14. When the cooking time is completed, press "Start/Stop" to stop cooking and open the lid.
15. Remove the ramekins and top each with mayonnaise.
16. Serve warm.

Nutritional Information per Serving:

Calories: 269 | Fat: 18.2g | Saturated Fat: 5.6g | Carbohydrates: 10.6g | Sugar: 2.7g | Protein: 16g

10. Spinach & Egg Bites

⏰ Prep Time 10 m | ⏰ Cooking Time 10 m | 2 Servings

Ingredients:

- 2 large eggs
- 2 tablespoons half-and-half
- 2 tablespoons frozen spinach, thawed
- 4 teaspoons mozzarella cheese, grated
- Salt and freshly ground black pepper, to taste

Instructions:

1. Grease 2 ramekins.
2. In each prepared ramekin, crack 1 egg.
3. Divide the half-and-half, spinach, cheese, salt and black pepper and each ramekin and gently stir to combine without breaking the yolks.
4. Arrange the "Crisper Basket" in the pot of Ninja Foodi Grill.
5. Close the Ninja Foodi Grill with lid and select "Air Crisp".
6. Set the temperature to 330 degrees F to preheat.
7. Press "Start/Stop" to begin preheating.
8. When the display shows "Add Food" open the lid and place the ramekins into the "Crisper Basket".
9. Close the Ninja Foodi Grill with lid and set the time for 10 minutes.
10. Press "Start/Stop" to begin cooking.
11. When the cooking time is completed, press "Start/Stop" to stop cooking and open the lid.
12. Serve hot.

Nutritional Information per Serving:

Calories: 251 | Fat: 16.7g | Saturated Fat: 8.6g | Carbohydrates: 3.1g | Sugar: 0.4g | Protein: 22.8g

11. Bacon & Egg Cups

⏰ Prep Time 10 m | ⏰ Cooking Time 8 m | 2 Servings

Ingredients:
- 1 cooked bacon slice, chopped
- 2 eggs
- 2 tablespoons milk
- 1 teaspoon marinara sauce
- 1 tablespoon Parmesan cheese, grated
- 1 tablespoon fresh parsley, chopped

Instructions:
1. Divide the bacon in 2 ramekins.
2. Crack 1 egg in each ramekin over bacon.
3. Place the milk over each egg evenly and sprinkle with black pepper.
4. Top with the marinara sauce, followed by the Parmesan cheese.
5. Arrange the "Crisper Basket" in the pot of Ninja Foodi Grill.
6. Close the Ninja Foodi Grill with lid and select "Air Crisp".
7. Set the temperature to 355 degrees F to preheat.
8. Press "Start/Stop" to begin preheating.
9. When the display shows "Add Food" open the lid and place the ramekins into the "Crisper Basket".
10. Close the Ninja Foodi Grill with lid and set the time for 8 minutes.
11. Press "Start/Stop" to begin cooking.
12. When the cooking time is completed, press "Start/Stop" to stop cooking and open the lid.
13. Serve hot with the garnishing of parsley.

Nutritional Information per Serving:
Calories: 161 | Fat: 11.4g | Saturated Fat: 3.9g | Carbohydrates: 1.8g | Sugar: 1.3g | Protein: 12.5g

12. Cheese Omelet

⏰ Prep Time 10 m | ⏰ Cooking Time 15 m | 2 Servings

Ingredients:
- 4 eggs
- ¼ teaspoon low-sodium soy sauce
- Ground black pepper, to taste
- 1 teaspoon butter
- 1 medium yellow onion, sliced
- ¼ cup Monterrey Jack cheese, grated

Instructions:
1. In a bowl, add the eggs, soy sauce and black pepper and beat well. Set aside.
2. In a frying pan, heat the oil over medium heat and cook the onion for about 8-10 minutes, stirring occasionally.
3. Remove from the heat and set aside to cool slightly.
4. Place the cooked onion into a small baking pan.
5. Place the egg mixture over onion slices, followed by the cheese evenly.
6. Arrange the "Crisper Basket" in the pot of Ninja Foodi Grill.
7. Close the Ninja Foodi Grill with lid and select "Air Crisp".
8. Set the temperature to 355 degrees F to preheat.
9. Press "Start/Stop" to begin preheating.
10. When the display shows "Add Food" open the lid and place the baking pan into the "Crisper Basket".
11. Close the Ninja Foodi Grill with lid and set the time for 5 minutes.
12. Press "Start/Stop" to begin cooking.
13. When the cooking time is completed, press "Start/Stop" to stop cooking and open the lid.
14. Cut the omelet into equal-sized wedges and serve hot.

Nutritional Information per Serving:
Calories: 165 | Fat: 10.6g | Saturated Fat: 3.9g | Carbohydrates: 5.9g | Sugar: 3.1g | Protein: 11.8g

13. Cheddar & Cream Omelet

⏰ Prep Time 10 m | ⏰ Cooking Time 8 m | 2 Servings

Ingredients:
- 4 eggs
- ¼ cup cream
- Salt and freshly ground black pepper, to taste
- ¼ cup cheddar cheese, grated

Instructions:
1. Lightly grease a 6x3-inch baking pan.
2. In a bowl, add the eggs, cream, salt, and black pepper and beat well.
3. Place the egg mixture into a greased 6x3-inch pan.
4. Arrange the "Crisper Basket" in the pot of Ninja Foodi Grill.
5. Close the Ninja Foodi Grill with lid and select "Air Crisp".
6. Set the temperature to 350 degrees F to preheat.
7. Press "Start/Stop" to begin preheating.
8. When the display shows "Add Food" open the lid and place the pan into the "Crisper Basket".
9. Close the Ninja Foodi Grill with lid and set the time for 8 minutes.
10. Press "Start/Stop" to begin cooking.
11. After 4 minutes of cooking, sprinkle the omelet with cheese evenly.
12. When the cooking time is completed, press "Start/Stop" to stop cooking and open the lid.
13. Cut the omelet into equal-sized wedges and serve hot.

Nutritional Information per Serving:
Calories: 202 | Fat: 15.1g | Saturated Fat: 6.8g | Carbohydrates: 1.8g | Sugar: 1.4g | Protein: 14.8g

14. Mushroom & Pepperoncini Omelet

⏰ Prep Time 15 m | ⏱ Cooking Time 20 m | 2 Servings

Ingredients:

- 3 large eggs
- ¼ cup milk
- Salt and freshly ground black pepper, to taste
- ½ cup cheddar cheese, shredded
- ¼ cup cooked mushrooms, chopped
- 3 pepperoncini peppers, sliced thinly
- ½ tablespoon scallion, sliced thinly

Instructions:

1. In a bowl, add the eggs, milk, salt and black pepper and beat well.
2. Place the mixture into a greased baking pan.
3. Add the remaining ingredients and stir to combine.
4. Arrange the "Crisper Basket" in the pot of Ninja Foodi Grill.
5. Close the Ninja Foodi Grill with lid and select "Bake".
6. Set the temperature to 350 degrees F to preheat.
7. Press "Start/Stop" to begin preheating.
8. When the display shows "Add Food" open the lid and place the pan into the "Crisper Basket".
9. Close the Ninja Foodi Grill with lid and set the time for 20 minutes.
10. Press "Start/Stop" to begin cooking.
11. When the cooking time is completed, press "Start/Stop" to stop cooking and open the lid.
12. Cut into equal-sized wedges and serve hot.

Nutritional Information per Serving:

Calories: 254 | Fat: 7.5g | Saturated Fat: 8.7g | Carbohydrates: 7.3g | Sugar: 3.8g | Protein: 8.2g

15. Zucchini Omelet

⏰ Prep Time 15 m | ⏱ Cooking Time 15 m | 2 Servings

Ingredients:

- 1 teaspoon butter
- 1 zucchini, julienned
- 4 eggs
- ¼ teaspoon fresh basil, chopped
- ¼ teaspoon red pepper flakes, crushed
- Salt and freshly ground black pepper, to taste

Instructions:

1. In a frying pan, melt the butter over medium heat and cook the zucchini for about 4-5 minutes.
2. Remove from the heat and set aside to cool slightly.
3. Meanwhile, in a bowl, add the eggs, basil, red pepper flakes, salt and black pepper and beat until well combined.
4. Place the egg mixture over zucchini and gently stir to combine.
5. Place the mixture into a baking pan..
6. Arrange the "Crisper Basket" in the pot of Ninja Foodi Grill.
7. Close the Ninja Foodi Grill with lid and select "Air Crisp".
8. Set the temperature to 355 degrees F to preheat.
9. Press "Start/Stop" to begin preheating.
10. When the display shows "Add Food" open the lid and place the pan into the "Crisper Basket".
11. Close the Ninja Foodi Grill with lid and set the time for 10 minutes.
12. Press "Start/Stop" to begin cooking.
13. When the cooking time is completed, press "Start/Stop" to stop cooking and open the lid.
14. Cut into equal-sized wedges and serve hot.

Nutritional Information per Serving:

Calories: 159 | Fat: 10.9g | Saturated Fat: 4g | Carbohydrates: 4.1g | Sugar: 2.4g | Protein: 12.3g

16. Chicken Omelet

⏰ Prep Time 15 m | ⏰ Cooking Time 16 m | 2 Servings

Ingredients:

- 1 teaspoon butter
- 1 small yellow onion, chopped
- ½ jalapeño pepper, seeded and chopped
- ¼ cup cooked chicken, shredded
- 3 eggs
- Salt and freshly ground black pepper, to taste

Instructions:

1. In a frying pan, melt the butter over medium heat and cook the zucchini for about 4-5 minutes.
2. Add the jalapeño pepper and cook for about 1 minute.
3. Remove from the heat and stir in the cooked chicken.
4. Set aside to cool slightly.
5. Meanwhile, in a bowl, add the eggs, salt, and black pepper and beat well.
6. Place the mixture into a baking pan..
7. Arrange the "Crisper Basket" in the pot of Ninja Foodi Grill.
8. Close the Ninja Foodi Grill with lid and select "Air Crisp".
9. Set the temperature to 355 degrees F to preheat.
10. Press "Start/Stop" to begin preheating.
11. When the display shows "Add Food" open the lid and place the pan into the "Crisper Basket".
12. Close the Ninja Foodi Grill with lid and set the time for 8 minutes.
13. Press "Start/Stop" to begin cooking.
14. When the cooking time is completed, press "Start/Stop" to stop cooking and open the lid.
15. Cut into equal-sized wedges and serve hot.

Nutritional Information per Serving:
Calories: 153 | Fat: 9.1g | Saturated Fat: 3.4g | Carbohydrates: 4g | Sugar: 2.1g | Protein: 13.8g

17. Pepperoni Omelet

⏰ Prep Time 10 m | ⏰ Cooking Time 12 m | 2 Servings

Ingredients:

- 3 eggs
- 2 tablespoons milk
- Pinch of salt
- Ground black pepper, to taste
- 8-10 turkey pepperoni slices

Instructions:

1. In a bowl, crack the eggs and beat well.
2. Add the remaining ingredients and gently stir to combine.
3. Place the mixture into a baking pan..
4. Arrange the "Crisper Basket" in the pot of Ninja Foodi Grill.
5. Close the Ninja Foodi Grill with lid and select "Air Crisp".
6. Set the temperature to 355 degrees F to preheat.
7. Press "Start/Stop" to begin preheating.
8. When the display shows "Add Food" open the lid and place the pan into the "Crisper Basket".
9. Close the Ninja Foodi Grill with lid and set the time for 12 minutes.
10. Press "Start/Stop" to begin cooking.
11. When the cooking time is completed, press "Start/Stop" to stop cooking and open the lid.
12. Cut into equal-sized wedges and serve hot.

Nutritional Information per Serving:
Calories: 118 | Fat: 7.8g | Saturated Fat: 2.6g | Carbohydrates: 1.3g | Sugar: 1.2g | Protein: 10.8g

18. Sausage & Bacon Omelet

⏰ Prep Time 10 m | ⏰ Cooking Time 10 m | 2 Servings

Ingredients:

- 4 eggs
- 1 bacon slice, chopped
- 2 sausages, chopped
- 1 yellow onion, chopped

Instructions:

1. In a bowl, crack the eggs and beat well.
2. Add the remaining ingredients and gently stir to combine.
3. Place the mixture into a baking pan..
4. Arrange the "Crisper Basket" in the pot of Ninja Foodi Grill.
5. Close the Ninja Foodi Grill with lid and select "Air Crisp".
6. Set the temperature to 320 degrees F to preheat.
7. Press "Start/Stop" to begin preheating.
8. When the display shows "Add Food" open the lid and place the pan into the "Crisper Basket".
9. Close the Ninja Foodi Grill with lid and set the time for 10 minutes.
10. Press "Start/Stop" to begin cooking.
11. When the cooking time is completed, press "Start/Stop" to stop cooking and open the lid.
12. Cut into equal-sized wedges and serve hot.

Nutritional Information per Serving:

Calories: 508 | Fat: 38.4g | Saturated Fat: 12.3g | Carbohydrates: 6g | Sugar: 3g | Protein: 33.2g

19. Tofu Omelet

⏰ Prep Time 15 m | ⏰ Cooking Time 10 m | 2 Servings

Ingredients:

- 1 teaspoon cornstarch
- 2 teaspoons water
- 3 eggs
- 2 teaspoons red boat fish sauce
- 1 teaspoon olive oil
- Ground black pepper, to taste
- 8 ounces silken tofu, pressed and chopped

Instructions:

1. In a large bowl, dissolve cornstarch in water.
2. Add the eggs, fish sauce, oil and black pepper and beat well.
3. In the bottom of a greased baking pan, place tofu and top with the egg mixture.
4. Arrange the "Crisper Basket" in the pot of Ninja Foodi Grill.
5. Close the Ninja Foodi Grill with lid and select "Air Crisp".
6. Set the temperature to 390 degrees F to preheat.
7. Press "Start/Stop" to begin preheating.
8. When the display shows "Add Food" open the lid and place the pan into the "Crisper Basket".
9. Close the Ninja Foodi Grill with lid and set the time for 10 minutes.
10. Press "Start/Stop" to begin cooking.
11. When the cooking time is completed, press "Start/Stop" to stop cooking and open the lid.
12. Cut into equal-sized wedges and serve hot.

Nutritional Information per Serving:

Calories: 195 | Fat: 12g | Saturated Fat: 2.8g | Carbohydrates: 4.5g | Sugar: 2g | Protein: 17.5g

20. Sausage & Scallion Frittata

⏰ Prep Time 10 m | ⏰ Cooking Time 20 m | 2 Servings

Ingredients:

- ¼ pound cooked turkey sausage, crumbled
- ½ cup Cheddar cheese, shredded
- 4 eggs, beaten lightly
- 2 scallions, chopped
- Pinch of cayenne pepper

Instructions:

1. In a bowl, add the sausage, cheese, eggs, scallion and cayenne and mix until well combined.
2. Place the mixture into a greased 6x2-inch cake pan.
3. Arrange the "Crisper Basket" in the pot of Ninja Foodi Grill.
4. Close the Ninja Foodi Grill with lid and select "Air Crisp".
5. Set the temperature to 360 degrees F to preheat.
6. Press "Start/Stop" to begin preheating.
7. When the display shows "Add Food" open the lid and place the pan into the "Crisper Basket".
8. Close the Ninja Foodi Grill with lid and set the time for 20 minutes.
9. Press "Start/Stop" to begin cooking.
10. When the cooking time is completed, press "Start/Stop" to stop cooking and open the lid.
11. Cut into equal-sized wedges and serve hot.

Nutritional Information per Serving:
Calories: 437 | Fat: 34.2g | Saturated Fat: 13.9g | Carbohydrates: 2.2g | Sugar: 1.2g | Protein: 29.4g

21. Pancetta & Spinach Frittata

⏰ Prep Time 10 m | ⏰ Cooking Time 15 m | 2 Servings

Ingredients:

- ¼ cup pancetta
- ½ tomato, cubed
- ¼ cup fresh baby spinach
- 3 eggs
- Salt and freshly ground black pepper, to taste
- ¼ cup Parmesan cheese, grated

Instructions:

1. Heat a greased frying pan over medium heat and cook the pancetta and tomato and tomato and cook for about 5 minutes.
2. Add the spinach and cook for about 1-2 minutes.
3. Remove from the heat and set aside to cool slightly.
4. Meanwhile, in a small bowl, add the eggs, salt and black pepper and beat well.
5. Place the pancetta mixture into a baking pan evenly and top with the egg mixture, followed by the cheese.
6. Arrange the "Crisper Basket" in the pot of Ninja Foodi Grill.
7. Close the Ninja Foodi Grill with lid and select "Air Crisp".
8. Set the temperature to 355 degrees F to preheat.
9. Press "Start/Stop" to begin preheating.
10. When the display shows "Add Food" open the lid and place the pan into the "Crisper Basket".
11. Close the Ninja Foodi Grill with lid and set the time for 8 minutes.
12. Press "Start/Stop" to begin cooking.
13. When the cooking time is completed, press "Start/Stop" to stop cooking and open the lid.
14. Cut into equal-sized wedges and serve hot.

Nutritional Information per Serving:
Calories: 371 | Fat: 26.4g | Saturated Fat: 11g | Carbohydrates: 3.7g | Sugar: 0.9g | Protein: 31.1g

22. Trout Frittata

⏰ Prep Time 15 m | ⏰ Cooking Time 25 m | 4 Servings

Ingredients:

- 2 tablespoons olive oil
- 1 onion, sliced
- 6 eggs
- ½ tablespoon horseradish sauce
- 2 tablespoons crème fraiche
- 2 hot-smoked trout fillets, chopped
- ¼ cup fresh dill, chopped

Instructions:

1. In a frying pan, heat the oil over medium heat and cook the zucchini for about 4-5 minutes.
2. Remove from the heat and set aside to cool slightly.
3. Meanwhile, in a bowl, add the eggs, horseradish sauce, and crème fraiche and mix well.
4. Transfer the onion mixture into a baking pan. and top with the egg mixture, followed by trout.
5. Arrange the "Crisper Basket" in the pot of Ninja Foodi Grill.
6. Close the Ninja Foodi Grill with lid and select "Air Crisp".
7. Set the temperature to 320 degrees F to preheat.
8. Press "Start/Stop" to begin preheating.
9. When the display shows "Add Food" open the lid and place the pan into the "Crisper Basket".
10. Close the Ninja Foodi Grill with lid and set the time for 20 minutes.
11. Press "Start/Stop" to begin cooking.
12. When the cooking time is completed, press "Start/Stop" to stop cooking and open the lid.
13. Cut into equal-sized wedges and serve hot.

Nutritional Information per Serving:

Calories: 288 | Fat: 19.2g | Saturated Fat: 4.4g | Carbohydrates: 5.1g | Sugar: 1.8g | Protein: 24.4g

23. Spinach & Tomato Frittata

⏰ Prep Time 15 m | ⏰ Cooking Time 30 m | 6 Servings

Ingredients:

- 10 large eggs
- Salt and freshly ground black pepper, to taste
- 1 (5-ounce) bag baby spinach
- 2 cups grape tomatoes, halved
- 4 scallions, sliced thinly
- 8 ounces feta cheese, crumbled
- 3 tablespoons hot olive oil

Instructions:

1. In a bowl, place the eggs, salt and black pepper and beat well.
2. Add the spinach, tomatoes, scallions and feta cheese and gently stir to combine.
3. Spread the oil in a baking pan and top with the spinach mixture.
4. Arrange the "Crisper Basket" in the pot of Ninja Foodi Grill.
5. Close the Ninja Foodi Grill with lid and select "Bake".
6. Set the temperature to 350 degrees F to preheat.
7. Press "Start/Stop" to begin preheating.
8. When the display shows "Add Food" open the lid and place the pan into the "Crisper Basket".
9. Close the Ninja Foodi Grill with lid and set the time for 30 minutes.
10. Press "Start/Stop" to begin cooking.
11. When the cooking time is completed, press "Start/Stop" to stop cooking and open the lid.
12. Cut into equal-sized wedges and serve hot.

Nutritional Information per Serving:

Calories: 298 | Fat: 23.6g | Saturated Fat: 9.3g | Carbohydrates: 6.1g | Sugar: 4.1g | Protein: 17.2g

24. Bacon & Mushroom Frittata

⏱ Prep Time 15 m | ⏱ Cooking Time 14 m | 2 Servings

Ingredients:

- 1 bacon slice, chopped
- 6 cherry tomatoes, halved
- 6 fresh mushrooms, sliced
- Salt and freshly ground black pepper, to taste
- 3 eggs
- 1 tablespoon fresh parsley, chopped
- ½ cup Parmesan cheese, grated

Instructions:

1. In a baking pan, add the bacon, tomatoes, mushrooms, salt, and black pepper and mix well.
2. Arrange the "Crisper Basket" in the pot of Ninja Foodi Grill.
3. Close the Ninja Foodi Grill with lid and select "Air Crisp".
4. Set the temperature to 320 degrees F to preheat.
5. Press "Start/Stop" to begin preheating.
6. When the display shows "Add Food" open the lid and place the pan into the "Crisper Basket".
7. Close the Ninja Foodi Grill with lid and set the time for 14 minutes.
8. Press "Start/Stop" to begin cooking.
9. Meanwhile, in a bowl, add the eggs and beat well.
10. Add in the parsley and cheese and mix well.
11. After 6 minutes, top the bacon mixture with egg mixture evenly.
12. When the cooking time is completed, press "Start/Stop" to stop cooking and open the lid.
13. Cut into equal-sized wedges and serve hot.

Nutritional Information per Serving:

Calories: 489 | Fat: 35.8g | Saturated Fat: 15.1g | Carbohydrates: 7.5g | Sugar: 2.1g | Protein: 39.6g

25. Mini Tomato Quiches

⏱ Prep Time 10 m | ⏱ Cooking Time 30 m | 2 Servings

Ingredients:

- 4 eggs
- ¼ cup onion, chopped
- ½ cup tomatoes, chopped
- ½ cup milk
- 1 cup Gouda cheese, shredded
- Salt, to taste

Instructions:

1. In a large ramekin, add all the ingredients and mix well.
2. Arrange the "Crisper Basket" in the pot of Ninja Foodi Grill.
3. Close the Ninja Foodi Grill with lid and select "Air Crisp".
4. Set the temperature to 340 degrees F to preheat.
5. Press "Start/Stop" to begin preheating.
6. When the display shows "Add Food" open the lid and place the ramekin into the "Crisper Basket".
7. Close the Ninja Foodi Grill with lid and set the time for 30 minutes.
8. Press "Start/Stop" to begin cooking.
9. When the cooking time is completed, press "Start/Stop" to stop cooking and open the lid.
10. Serve hot.

Nutritional Information per Serving:

Calories: 247 | Fat: 16.1g | Saturated Fat: 7.5g | Carbohydrates: 7.3g | Sugar: 5.2g | Protein: 18.6g

POULTRY RECIPES

26. Spiced Cornish Hen

⏰ Prep Time 15 m | ⏰ Cooking Time 40 m | 4 Servings

Ingredients:

- 1 teaspoon dried rosemary, crushed
- 1 teaspoon dried thyme, crushed
- 1 teaspoon poultry seasoning
- 1 teaspoon garlic powder
- 1 teaspoon smoked paprika
- Salt and freshly ground black pepper, to taste
- 2 (1¼-pound) Cornish hens
- 2-3 tablespoons olive oil
- 1 lemon, cut into slices

Instructions:

1. In a small bowl, mix together the dried herbs, poultry seasoning, spices, salt and black pepper.
2. Brush both hens with oil and then sprinkle with herb mixture evenly.
3. Arrange the greased "Crisper Basket" in the pot of Ninja Foodi Grill.
4. Close the Ninja Foodi Grill with lid and select "Air Crisp".
5. Set the temperature to 350 degrees F to preheat.
6. Press "Start/Stop" to begin preheating.
7. When the display shows "Add Food" open the lid and place the lemon slices into the "Crisper Basket".
8. Arrange both hens over lemon slices.
9. Close the Ninja Foodi Grill with lid and set the time for 40 minutes.
10. Press "Start/Stop" to begin cooking.
11. Flip the hens once after 20 minutes.
12. When cooking time is completed, press "Start/Stop" to stop cooking and open the lid.
13. Place the hens onto a cutting board for about 15 minutes.
14. Cut each hen into desired sized pieces and serve.

Nutritional Information per Serving:
Calories: 448 | Fat: 18.2g | Saturated Fat: 3.9g | Carbohydrates: 1.8g | Sugar: 0.3g | Protein: 66.4g

27. Herbed Cornish Hen

⏰ Prep Time 15 m | ⏰ Cooking Time 16 m | 4 Servings

Ingredients:

- ½ cup olive oil
- 1 teaspoon fresh rosemary, chopped
- 1 teaspoon fresh thyme, chopped
- 1 teaspoon fresh lemon zest, grated finely
- ¼ teaspoon sugar
- ¼ teaspoon red pepper flakes, crushed
- Salt and freshly ground black pepper, to taste
- 2 pounds Cornish game hen, backbone removed and halved

Instructions:

1. In a large bowl, mix well all ingredients except hen portions.
2. Add the hen portions and coat with marinade generously.
3. Cover and refrigerator for about 2-24 hours.
4. In a strainer, place the hen portions to drain any liquid.
5. Arrange the greased "Crisper Basket" in the pot of Ninja Foodi Grill.
6. Close the Ninja Foodi Grill with lid and select "Air Crisp".
7. Set the temperature to 390 degrees F to preheat.
8. Press "Start/Stop" to begin preheating.
9. When the display shows "Add Food" open the lid and place the hen portions into the "Crisper Basket".
10. Close the Ninja Foodi Grill with lid and set the time for 16 minutes.
11. Press "Start/Stop" to begin cooking.
12. When cooking time is completed, press "Start/Stop" to stop cooking and open the lid.
13. Place the hen portions onto a cutting board.
14. Cut each portion in 2 pieces and serve hot.

Nutritional Information per Serving:
Calories: 681 | Fat: 57.4g | Saturated Fat: 12.7g | Carbohydrates: 0.8g | Sugar: 0.3g | Protein: 38.2g

28. Spicy Whole Chicken

⏰ Prep Time 15 m | ⏰ Cooking Time 1 h | 4 Servings

Ingredients:

- 2 teaspoons dried thyme
- 2 teaspoons paprika
- 1 teaspoon cayenne pepper
- 1 teaspoon ground white pepper
- 1 teaspoon onion powder
- 1 teaspoon garlic powder
- 1 (5-pound) whole chicken, necks and giblets removed
- 3 tablespoons oil
- Salt and freshly ground black pepper, to taste

Instructions:

1. In a bowl, mix together the thyme and spices.
2. Coat the chicken with oil and then rub it with spice mixture.
3. Season the chicken with salt and black pepper evenly.
4. Arrange the greased "Crisper Basket" in the pot of Ninja Foodi Grill.
5. Close the Ninja Foodi Grill with lid and select "Air Crisp".
6. Set the temperature to 350 degrees F to preheat.
7. Press "Start/Stop" to begin preheating.
8. When the display shows "Add Food" open the lid and place the chicken into the "Crisper Basket".
9. Close the Ninja Foodi Grill with lid and set the time for 1 hour.
10. Press "Start/Stop" to begin cooking.
11. Flip the chicken once after 30 minutes.
12. When cooking time is completed, press "Start/Stop" to stop cooking and open the lid.
13. Place the chicken onto a cutting board for about 10 minutes before carving.
14. Cut the chicken into desired sized pieces and serve.

Nutritional Information per Serving:
Calories: 590 | Fat: 26.3g | Saturated Fat: 6.5g | Carbohydrates: 1.3g | Sugar: 0.3g | Protein: 82.3g

29. Herbed Whole Chicken

Prep Time 15 m | Cooking Time 1 h 10 m | 6 Servings

Ingredients:
- ¼ cup butter, softened
- 1 teaspoon dried rosemary, crushed
- 1 teaspoon dried basil, crushed
- 1 teaspoon dried oregano, crushed
- 1 teaspoon dried thyme, crushed
- 1 tablespoon garlic powder
- 1 tablespoon paprika
- 1 tablespoon ground cumin
- Salt and freshly ground black pepper, to taste
- 1 (3-pound) whole chicken, neck and giblets removed

Instructions:
1. In a bowl, add the butter, herbs, spices and salt and mix well.
2. Rub the chicken with spice mixture generously.
3. With kitchen twine, tie off wings and legs.
4. Arrange the chicken onto the greased baking pan.
5. Arrange the "Crisper Basket" in the pot of Ninja Foodi Grill.
6. Close the Ninja Foodi Grill with lid and select "Bake".
7. Set the temperature to 380 degrees F to preheat.
8. Press "Start/Stop" to begin preheating.
9. When the display shows "Add Food" open the lid and place the pan into the "Crisper Basket".
10. Close the Ninja Foodi Grill with lid and set the time for 70 minutes.
11. Press "Start/Stop" to begin cooking.
12. When the cooking time is completed, press "Start/Stop" to stop cooking and open the lid.
13. Place the chicken onto a platter for about 5-10 minutes before carving.
14. With a sharp knife, cut the chicken into desired sized pieces and serve.

Nutritional Information per Serving:
Calories: 434 | Fat: 15g | Saturated Fat: 6.9g | Carbohydrates: 2.5g | Sugar: 0.5g | Protein: 66.4g

30. Lemony Whole Chicken

⏰ Prep Time 15 m | ⏰ Cooking Time 1 h 29 m | 10 Servings

Ingredients:

- 1 (6-pound) whole chicken, necks and giblets removed
- Salt and freshly ground black pepper, to taste
- 3 fresh rosemary sprigs, divided
- 1 lemon, zested and cut into quarters
- 2 large onions, sliced,
- 4 cups chicken broth

Instructions:

1. Stuff the cavity of chicken with 2 rosemary sprigs and lemon quarters.
2. Season the chicken with salt and black pepper evenly.
3. Chop the remaining rosemary sprig and set aside.
4. Heat a greased large skillet over medium-high heat and cook the chicken for about 5-7 minutes per side.
5. Remove chicken from the skillet and place into a baking pan.
6. In the pot, place the onions and broth.
7. Sprinkle the chicken with reserved chopped rosemary and lemon zest.
8. Arrange the "Crisper Basket" in the pot of Ninja Foodi Grill.
9. Close the Ninja Foodi Grill with lid and select "Bake".
10. Set the temperature to 375 degrees F to preheat.
11. Press "Start/Stop" to begin preheating.
12. When the display shows "Add Food" open the lid and place the pan into the "Crisper Basket".
13. Close the Ninja Foodi Grill with lid and set the time for 75 minutes.
14. Press "Start/Stop" to begin cooking.
15. When the cooking time is completed, press "Start/Stop" to stop cooking and open the lid.
16. Place the chicken onto a platter for about 5-10 minutes before carving.
17. With a sharp knife, cut the chicken into desired sized pieces and serve.

Nutritional Information per Serving:
Calories: 545 | Fat: 20.8g | Saturated Fat: 5.7g | Carbohydrates: 3.3g | Sugar: 1.6g | Protein: 81g

31. Whole Chicken with Potatoes

⏰ Prep Time 15 m | ⏰ Cooking Time 1 h | 2 Servings

Ingredients:

- 1 (1½-pound) whole chicken
- Salt and freshly ground black pepper, to taste
- 1 tablespoon dried rosemary, crushed
- ½ pound small potatoes
- 1 tablespoon olive oil

Instructions:

1. Arrange the greased "Crisper Basket" in the pot of Ninja Foodi Grill.
2. Close the Ninja Foodi Grill with lid and select "Air Crisp".
3. Set the temperature to 390 degrees F to preheat.
4. Press "Start/Stop" to begin preheating.
5. Season the chicken with salt and black pepper and then rub with rosemary.
6. When the display shows "Add Food" open the lid and place the chicken into the "Crisper Basket".
7. Close the Ninja Foodi Grill with lid and set the time for 60 minutes.
8. Press "Start/Stop" to begin cooking.
9. Meanwhile, in a bowl, add the potatoes, oil, salt and black pepper and toss to coat well.
10. After 40 minutes of cooking, arrange the potatoes into the "Crisper Basket".
11. When the cooking time is completed, press "Start/Stop" to stop cooking and open the lid.
12. Place the chicken onto a cutting board for about 10 minutes.
13. Cut the chicken into desired sized pieces and serve alongside the potatoes.

Nutritional Information per Serving:

Calories: 782 | Fat: 49.9g | Saturated Fat: 13.3g | Carbohydrates: 18.9g | Sugar: 1.3g | Protein: 62.8g

32. Crispy Roasted Chicken

⏰ Prep Time 15 m | ⏰ Cooking Time 40 m | 8 Servings

Ingredients:

- 1 (3½-pound) whole chicken, cut into 8 pieces
- Salt and freshly ground black pepper, to taste
- 2 cups buttermilk
- 2 cups all-purpose flour
- 1 tablespoon ground mustard
- 1 tablespoon garlic powder
- 1 tablespoon onion powder
- 1 tablespoon paprika

Instructions:

1. Rub the chicken pieces with salt and black pepper.
2. In a large bowl, add the chicken pieces and buttermilk and refrigerate to marinate for at least 1 hour.
3. Meanwhile, in a large bowl, place the flour, mustard, spices, salt and black pepper and mix well.
4. Remove the chicken pieces from bowl and drip off the excess buttermilk.
5. Coat the chicken pieces with the flour mixture, shaking any excess off.
6. Arrange the greased "Crisper Basket" in the pot of Ninja Foodi Grill.
7. Close the Ninja Foodi Grill with lid and select "Air Crisp".
8. Set the temperature to 390 degrees F to preheat.
9. Press "Start/Stop" to begin preheating.
10. When the display shows "Add Food" open the lid and place the half of the chicken pieces into the "Crisper Basket".
11. Close the Ninja Foodi Grill with lid and set the time for 20 minutes.
12. Press "Start/Stop" to begin cooking.
13. When the cooking time is completed, press "Start/Stop" to stop cooking and open the lid.
14. Transfer the chicken pieces onto a platter.
15. Repeat with the remaining chicken pieces.
16. Serve immediately.

Nutritional Information per Serving:
Calories: 518 | Fat: 8.5g | Saturated Fat: 2.4g | Carbohydrates: 33.4g | Sugar: 4.3g | Protein: 72.6g

33. Spicy Chicken Legs

⏰ Prep Time 15 m | ⏰ Cooking Time 20 m | 4 Servings

Ingredients:

- 4 (8-ounce) chicken legs
- 3 tablespoons fresh lemon juice
- 3 teaspoons ginger paste
- 3 teaspoons garlic paste
- Salt, to taste
- 4 tablespoons plain yogurt
- 2 teaspoons red chili powder
- 1 teaspoon ground cumin
- 1 teaspoon ground coriander
- 1 teaspoon ground turmeric
- Ground black pepper, to taste

Instructions:

1. In a bowl, mix together the chicken legs, lemon juice, ginger, garlic and salt. Set aside for about 15 minutes.
2. Meanwhile, in another bowl, mix together the yogurt and spices.
3. Add the chicken legs and coat with the spice mixture generously.
4. Cover the bowl and refrigerate for at least 10-12 hours.
5. Arrange the greased "Crisper Basket" in the pot of Ninja Foodi Grill.
6. Close the Ninja Foodi Grill with lid and select "Air Crisp".
7. Set the temperature to 445 degrees F to preheat.
8. Press "Start/Stop" to begin preheating.
9. When the display shows "Add Food" open the lid and place the chicken legs into the "Crisper Basket".
10. Close the Ninja Foodi Grill with lid and set the time for 20 minutes.
11. Press "Start/Stop" to begin cooking.
12. When the cooking time is completed, press "Start/Stop" to stop cooking and open the lid.
13. Serve hot.

Nutritional Information per Serving:
Calories: 461 | Fat: 17.6g | Saturated Fat: 5g | Carbohydrates: 4.3g | Sugar: 1.5g | Protein: 67.1g

34. Crispy Chicken Legs

⏰ Prep Time 15 m | ⏰ Cooking Time 20 m | 3 Servings

Ingredients:

- 3 (8-ounce) chicken legs
- 1 cup buttermilk
- 2 cups white flour
- 1 teaspoon garlic powder
- 1 teaspoon onion powder
- 1 teaspoon ground cumin
- 1 teaspoon paprika
- Salt and freshly ground black pepper, to taste
- 1 tablespoon olive oil

Instructions:

1. In a bowl, place the chicken legs and buttermilk and refrigerate for about 2 hours.
2. In a shallow dish, mix together the flour and spices.
3. Remove the chicken from buttermilk.
4. Coat the chicken legs with flour mixture, then dip into buttermilk and finally, coat with the flour mixture again.
5. Arrange the greased "Crisper Basket" in the pot of Ninja Foodi Grill.
6. Close the Ninja Foodi Grill with lid and select "Air Crisp".
7. Set the temperature to 360 degrees F to preheat.
8. Press "Start/Stop" to begin preheating.
9. When the display shows "Add Food" open the lid and place the chicken legs into the "Crisper Basket".
10. Close the Ninja Foodi Grill with lid and set the time for 20 minutes.
11. Press "Start/Stop" to begin cooking.
12. When the cooking time is completed, press "Start/Stop" to stop cooking and open the lid.
13. Serve hot.

Nutritional Information per Serving:
Calories: 817 | Fat: 23.3g | Saturated Fat: 5.9g | Carbohydrates: 69.5g | Sugar: 4.7g | Protein: 77.4g

35. Sweet & Spicy Chicken Drumsticks

⏲ Prep Time 20 m | ⏲ Cooking Time 10 m | 4 Servings

Ingredients:

- 1 garlic clove, crushed
- 1 teaspoon cayenne pepper
- 1 teaspoon red chili powder
- 2 teaspoons sugar
- 1 tablespoon mustard
- Salt and freshly ground black pepper, to taste
- 1 tablespoon olive oil
- 4 (6-ounce) chicken drumsticks

Instructions:

1. In a bowl, mix together all ingredients except chicken drumsticks.
2. Rub the chicken with the oil mix and refrigerate to marinate for about 20-30 minutes.
3. Arrange the greased "Crisper Basket" in the pot of Ninja Foodi Grill.
4. Close the Ninja Foodi Grill with lid and select "Air Crisp".
5. Set the temperature to 390 degrees F to preheat.
6. Press "Start/Stop" to begin preheating.
7. When the display shows "Add Food" open the lid and place the chicken drumsticks into the "Crisper Basket".
8. Close the Ninja Foodi Grill with lid and set the time for 10 minutes.
9. Press "Start/Stop" to begin cooking.
10. After 10 minutes of cooking, set the temperature to 300 degrees F for 10 minutes.
11. When cooking time is completed, press "Start/Stop" to stop cooking and open the lid.
12. Serve hot.

Nutritional Information per Serving:
Calories: 343 | Fat: 14.2g | Saturated Fat: 3.1g | Carbohydrates: 3.8g | Sugar: 2.3g | Protein: 47.7g

36. Glazed Chicken Drumsticks

⏰ Prep Time 15 m | ⏰ Cooking Time 20 m | 4 Servings

Ingredients:

- ¼ cup Dijon mustard
- 1 tablespoon honey
- 2 tablespoons olive oil
- 1 tablespoon fresh thyme, minced
- ½ tablespoon fresh rosemary, minced
- Salt and freshly ground black pepper, to taste
- 4 (6-ounce) boneless chicken drumsticks

Instructions:

1. In a bowl, add all ingredients except the drumsticks and mix until well combined.
2. Add the drumsticks and coat with the mixture generously.
3. Refrigerate, covered to marinate overnight.
4. Arrange the lightly greased "Crisper Basket" in the pot of Ninja Foodi Grill.
5. Close the Ninja Foodi Grill with lid and select "Air Crisp".
6. Set the temperature to 320 degrees F to preheat.
7. Press "Start/Stop" to begin preheating.
8. When the display shows "Add Food" open the lid and place the chicken drumsticks into the "Crisper Basket".
9. Close the Ninja Foodi Grill with lid and set the time for 12 minutes.
10. Press "Start/Stop" to begin cooking.
11. After 12 minutes, flip the drumsticks and set the temperature to 390 degrees F for 8 minutes.
12. When the cooking time is completed, press "Start/Stop" to stop cooking and open the lid.
13. Serve hot.

Nutritional Information per Serving:
Calories: 377 | Fat: 17.5g | Saturated Fat: 3.7g | Carbohydrates: 5.9g | Sugar: 4.5g | Protein: 47.6g

37. Rosemary Chicken Thighs

⏱ Prep Time 10 m | ⏱ Cooking Time 20 m | 2 Servings

Ingredients:

- 2 (4-ounces) skinless, boneless chicken thighs
- 1 teaspoon fresh rosemary, minced
- Salt and freshly ground black pepper, to taste
- 2 tablespoons butter, melted

Instructions:

1. Rub the chicken thighs with salt and black pepper evenly and then, brush with melted butter.
2. Place the chicken thighs into the greased baking pan.
3. Arrange the "Crisper Basket" in the pot of Ninja Foodi Grill.
4. Close the Ninja Foodi Grill with lid and select "Bake".
5. Set the temperature to 450 degrees F to preheat.
6. Press "Start/Stop" to begin preheating.
7. When the display shows "Add Food" open the lid and place the pan into the "Crisper Basket".
8. Close the Ninja Foodi Grill with lid and set the time for 20 minutes.
9. Press "Start/Stop" to begin cooking.
10. When the cooking time is completed, press "Start/Stop" to stop cooking and open the lid.
11. Serve hot.

Nutritional Information per Serving:
Calories: 246 | Fat: 15.7g | Saturated Fat: 8.9g | Carbohydrates: 0.4g | Sugar: 0g | Protein: 25.5g

38. Lemony Chicken Thighs

⏱ Prep Time 10 m | ⏱ Cooking Time 20 m | 6 Servings

Ingredients:

- 6 (6-ounce) chicken thighs
- 2 tablespoons olive oil
- 2 tablespoons fresh lemon juice
- 1 tablespoon Italian seasoning
- Salt and freshly ground black pepper, to taste
- 1 lemon, sliced thinly

Instructions:

1. In a large bowl, add all the ingredients except for lemon slices and toss to coat well.
2. Refrigerate to marinate for 30 minutes to overnight.
3. Remove the chicken thighs and let any excess marinade drip off.
4. Arrange the "Crisper Basket" in the pot of Ninja Foodi Grill.
5. Close the Ninja Foodi Grill with lid and select "Air Crisp".
6. Set the temperature to 350 degrees F to preheat.
7. Press "Start/Stop" to begin preheating.
8. When the display shows "Add Food" open the lid and place the chicken thighs into the "Crisper Basket".
9. Close the Ninja Foodi Grill with lid and set the time for 20 minutes.
10. Press "Start/Stop" to begin cooking.
11. After 10 minutes of cooking, flip the chicken thighs.
12. When the cooking time is completed, press "Start/Stop" to stop cooking and open the lid.
13. Serve hot alongside the lemon slices.

Nutritional Information per Serving:
Calories: 372 | Fat: 18g | Saturated Fat: 4.3g | Carbohydrates: 0.6g | Sugar: 0.4g | Protein: 49.3g

39. Marinated Chicken Thighs

⏰ Prep Time 10 m | ⏰ Cooking Time 30 m | 4 Servings

Ingredients:

- 4 (6-ounce) bone-in, skin-on chicken thighs
- Salt and freshly ground black pepper, to taste
- ½ cup Italian salad dressing
- 1 teaspoon onion powder
- 1 teaspoon garlic powder

Instructions:

1. Season the chicken thighs with salt and black pepper evenly.
2. In a large bowl, add the chicken thighs and dressing and mix well.
3. Cover the bowl and refrigerate to marinate overnight.
4. Remove the chicken breast from the bowl and place onto a plate.
5. Sprinkle the chicken thighs with onion powder and garlic powder.
6. Arrange the "Crisper Basket" in the pot of Ninja Foodi Grill.
7. Close the Ninja Foodi Grill with lid and select "Air Crisp".
8. Set the temperature to 360 degrees F to preheat.
9. Press "Start/Stop" to begin preheating.
10. When the display shows "Add Food" open the lid and place the chicken thighs into the "Crisper Basket".
11. Close the Ninja Foodi Grill with lid and set the time for 30 minutes.
12. Press "Start/Stop" to begin cooking.
13. After 15 minutes of cooking, flip the chicken thighs.
14. When the cooking time is completed, press "Start/Stop" to stop cooking and open the lid.
15. Serve hot.

Nutritional Information per Serving:

Calories: 413 | Fat: 21g | Saturated Fat: 4.8g | Carbohydrates: 4.1g | Sugar: 2.8g | Protein: 49.5g

40. Spiced Chicken Breasts

⏰ Prep Time 10 m | ⏰ Cooking Time 35 m | 4 Servings

Ingredients:
- 1½ tablespoons smoked paprika
- 1 teaspoon ground cumin
- Salt and freshly ground black pepper, to taste
- 2 (12-ounce) bone-in, skin-on chicken breasts
- 1 tablespoon olive oil

Instructions:
1. In a small bowl, mix together the paprika, cumin, salt and black pepper.
2. Coat the chicken breasts with oil evenly and then season with the spice mixture generously.
3. Arrange the "Crisper Basket" in the pot of Ninja Foodi Grill.
4. Close the Ninja Foodi Grill with lid and select "Air Crisp".
5. Set the temperature to 375 degrees F to preheat.
6. Press "Start/Stop" to begin preheating.
7. When the display shows "Add Food" open the lid and place the chicken breasts into the "Crisper Basket".
8. Close the Ninja Foodi Grill with lid and set the time for 35 minutes.
9. Press "Start/Stop" to begin cooking.
10. When the cooking time is completed, press "Start/Stop" to stop cooking and open the lid.
11. Place the chicken breasts onto a cutting board for about 5 minutes.
12. Cut each breast in 2 equal-sized pieces and serve.

Nutritional Information per Serving:
Calories: 363 | Fat: 16.6 g | Saturated Fat: 4 g | Carbohydrates: 1.7 g | Sugar: 0.3 g | Protein: 49.7 g

BEEF, PORK AND LAMB RECIPES

41. Simple Filet Mignon

⏰ Prep Time 10 m | ⏰ Cooking Time 14 m | 2 Servings

Ingredients:
- 2 (6-ounces) filet mignon
- 1 tablespoon olive oil
- Salt and freshly ground black pepper, to taste

Instructions:
1. Coat both sides of filet with oil and then, season with salt and black pepper.
2. Place the filets onto a greased air fryer basket.
3. Arrange the greased "Crisper Basket" in the pot of Ninja Foodi Grill.
4. Close the Ninja Foodi Grill with lid and select "Air Crisp".
5. Set the temperature to 390 degrees F to preheat.
6. Press "Start/Stop" to begin preheating.
7. When the display shows "Add Food" open the lid and place the filets into the "Crisper Basket".
8. Close the Ninja Foodi Grill with lid and set the time for 14 minutes.
9. Press "Start/Stop" to begin cooking.
10. Flip the filets once halfway through.
11. When the cooking time is completed, press "Start/Stop" to stop cooking and open the lid.
12. Serve hot.

Nutritional Information per Serving:
Calories: 364|Fat: 18.2g|Saturated Fat: 5.3g|Carbohydrates: 0g|Sugar: 0g|Protein: 47.8g

42. Seasoned Filet Mignon

⏰ Prep Time 10 m | ⏰ Cooking Time 7 m | 4 Servings

Ingredients:
- 4 (8-ounce) filet mignon
- ¼ cup olive oil
- 2 tablespoons steak seasoning
- 1 tablespoon salt

Instructions:
1. Coat both sides of each filet mignon with oil and then rub with steak seasoning and salt.
2. Arrange the greased "Grill Grate" in the pot of Ninja Foodi Grill.
3. Close the Ninja Foodi Grill with lid and select "Grill" to "High" to preheat.
4. With your hands, gently press down each fillet mignon.
5. Press "Start/Stop" to begin preheating.
6. When the display shows "Add Food" open the lid and place the filets onto the "Grill Grate".
7. Close the Ninja Foodi Grill with lid and set the time for 8 minutes.
8. With your hands, gently press down each filet.
9. Press "Start/Stop" to begin cooking.
10. After 4 minutes, flip the filets.
11. When the cooking time is completed, press "Start/Stop" to stop cooking and open the lid.
12. Transfer the filets onto a platter for about 5 minutes before serving.

Nutritional Information per Serving:
Calories: 425|Fat: 16.7g|Saturated Fat: 6.1g|Carbohydrates: 0.8g|Sugar: 0.1g|Protein: 63.9g

43. Seasoned Flank Steak

⏰ Prep Time 10 m | ⏰ Cooking Time 30 m | 6 Servings

Ingredients:

- 2 pounds flank steak
- 3 tablespoons taco seasoning rub

Instructions:

1. Rub the steak with taco seasoning evenly.
2. Place the steak into a greased baking pan.
3. Arrange the "Crisper Basket" in the pot of Ninja Foodi Grill.
4. Close the Ninja Foodi Grill with lid and select "Bake".
5. Set the temperature to 425 degrees F to preheat.
6. Press "Start/Stop" to begin preheating.
7. When the display shows "Add Food" open the lid and place the pan into the "Crisper Basket".
8. Close the Ninja Foodi Grill with lid and set the time for 30 minutes.
9. Press "Start/Stop" to begin cooking.
10. When the cooking time is completed, press "Start/Stop" to stop cooking and open the lid.
11. Place the steak onto a cutting board for about 10-15 minutes before slicing.
12. With a sharp knife, cut the steak into desired sized slices and serve.

Nutritional Information per Serving:
Calories: 308 | Fat: 12.6g | Saturated Fat: 5.2g | Carbohydrates: 3g | Sugar: 0.8g | Protein: 42.1g

44. Sweet & Sour Flank Steak

⏰ Prep Time 15 m | ⏰ Cooking Time 20 m | 4 Servings

Ingredients:

- 1 pound flank steak, sliced thinly
- 2 tablespoons flour
- ½ cup low-sodium soy sauce
- ½ cup sugar
- 2 tablespoons balsamic vinegar
- 1 garlic clove, crushed
- 1 teaspoon fresh ginger, grated
- ½ teaspoon red pepper flakes
- 1 tablespoon cornstarch
- 1 tablespoon water

Instructions:

1. Sprinkle the steak slices with flour evenly.
2. Arrange the greased "Crisper Basket" in the pot of Ninja Foodi Grill.
3. Close the Ninja Foodi Grill with lid and select "Air Crisp".
4. Set the temperature to 390 degrees F to preheat.
5. Press "Start/Stop" to begin preheating.
6. When the display shows "Add Food" open the lid and place the steak slices into the "Crisper Basket".
7. Close the Ninja Foodi Grill with lid and set the time for 20 minutes.
8. Press "Start/Stop" to begin cooking.
9. Flip the steak slices once halfway through.
10. Meanwhile, for sauce: in pan, add the remaining ingredients except for cornstarch and water and mix well.
11. Place the pan over medium heat and bring to a gentle boil.
12. In a bowl, dissolve the cornstarch in water.
13. Add the cornstarch mixture into the pan, stirring continuously.
14. Cook for about 1-2 minutes, stirring continuously.
15. Remove from the heat and transfer the sauce into a large bowl.
16. When the cooking time is completed, press "Start/Stop" to stop cooking and open the lid.
17. Place the steak slices into a bowl of sauce and mix well.
18. Serve immediately.

Nutritional Information per Serving:
Calories: 351 | Fat: 9.5g | Saturated Fat: 3.9g | Carbohydrates: 32.6g | Sugar: 27.1g | Protein: 34.1g

45. Crispy Sirloin Steaks

⏰ Prep Time 15 m | ⏰ Cooking Time 14 m | 3 Servings

Ingredients:

- ½ cup flour
- Salt and freshly ground black pepper, to taste
- 2 eggs
- ¾ cup breadcrumbs
- 3 (6-ounce) sirloin steaks, pounded

Instructions:

1. In a shallow bowl, place the flour, salt and black pepper and mix well.
2. In a second shallow bowl, beat the eggs.
3. In a third shallow bowl, place the breadcrumbs.
4. Coat the steak with flour, then dip into eggs, and finally coat with the panko mixture.
5. Arrange the greased "Crisper Basket" in the pot of Ninja Foodi Grill.
6. Close the Ninja Foodi Grill with lid and select "Air Crisp".
7. Set the temperature to 360 degrees F to preheat.
8. Press "Start/Stop" to begin preheating.
9. When the display shows "Add Food" open the lid and place the steaks into the "Crisper Basket".
10. Close the Ninja Foodi Grill with lid and set the time for 14 minutes.
11. Press "Start/Stop" to begin cooking.
12. When the cooking time is completed, press "Start/Stop" to stop cooking and open the lid.
13. Serve hot.

Nutritional Information per Serving:
Calories: 540 | Fat: 15.2g | Saturated Fat: 5.3g | Carbohydrates: 35.6g | Sugar: 2g | Protein: 61g

46. Buttered Striploin Steak

⏰ Prep Time 10 m | ⏰ Cooking Time 12 m | 2 Servings

Ingredients:

- 2 (7-ounce) striploin steaks
- 1½ tablespoons butter, softened
- Salt and freshly ground black pepper, to taste

Instructions:

1. Coat each steak evenly with butter and then season with salt and black pepper.
2. Arrange the greased "Crisper Basket" in the pot of Ninja Foodi Grill.
3. Close the Ninja Foodi Grill with lid and select "Air Crisp".
4. Set the temperature to 392 degrees F to preheat.
5. Press "Start/Stop" to begin preheating.
6. When the display shows "Add Food" open the lid and place the steaks into the "Crisper Basket".
7. Close the Ninja Foodi Grill with lid and set the time for 12 minutes.
8. Press "Start/Stop" to begin cooking.
9. When the cooking time is completed, press "Start/Stop" to stop cooking and open the lid.
10. Serve hot.

Nutritional Information per Serving:
Calories: 563 | Fat: 35.7g | Saturated Fat: 16.3g | Carbohydrates: 0g | Sugar: 0g | Protein: 56.9g

47. Vinegar London Broil Steak

⏰ Prep Time 15 m | ⏰ Cooking Time 7 m | 5 Servings

Ingredients:

- 1½ pounds London broil steak, trimmed
- ¼ cup red wine vinegar
- 1 tablespoon olive oil
- 1 tablespoon Worcestershire sauce
- 2 garlic cloves, minced
- 1-2 teaspoons fresh rosemary, chopped
- 1 teaspoon dried thyme
- 1½ tablespoons spicy mustard
- 1 teaspoon onion powder
- Salt and freshly ground black pepper, to taste

Instructions:

1. With a meat mallet, pound each side of steak slightly.
2. In a large plastic, sealable bag, place the remaining ingredients and mix.
3. Place the steak in bag and seal the bag.
4. Shake the bag vigorously to coat well.
5. Refrigerate to marinate for about 2-4 hours.
6. Remove the steak from the bag and set aside at room temperature for about 30 minutes.
7. Arrange the greased "Grill Grate" in the pot of Ninja Foodi Grill.
8. Close the Ninja Foodi Grill with lid and select "Grill" to "Max" to preheat.
9. Press "Start/Stop" to begin preheating.
10. When the display shows "Add Food" open the lid and place the steak onto the "Grill Grate".
11. With your hands, gently press down the steak.
12. Close the Ninja Foodi Grill with lid and set the time for 7 minutes.
13. Press "Start/Stop" to begin cooking.
14. After 4 minutes of cooking, flip the steak.
15. When the cooking time is completed, press "Start/Stop" to stop cooking and open the lid.
16. Place the steak onto a cutting board for about 10-15 minutes before slicing.
17. With a sharp knife, cut the steak into desired sized slices and serve.

Nutritional Information per Serving:
Calories: 344 | Fat: 16.9g | Saturated Fat: 5.4g | Carbohydrates: 3g | Sugar: 1.1g | Protein: 42.1g

48. Herbed Beef Roast

⏰ Prep Time 10 m | ⏰ Cooking Time 45 m | 5 Servings

Ingredients:

- 2 pounds beef roast
- 1 tablespoon olive oil
- 1 teaspoon dried rosemary, crushed
- 1 teaspoon dried thyme, crushed
- Salt, to taste

Instructions:

1. In a bowl, mix together the oil, herbs and salt.
2. Rub the roast with herb mixture generously.
3. Arrange the greased "Crisper Basket" in the pot of Ninja Foodi Grill.
4. Close the Ninja Foodi Grill with lid and select "Air Crisp".
5. Set the temperature to 360 degrees F to preheat.
6. Press "Start/Stop" to begin preheating.
7. When the display shows "Add Food" open the lid and place the roast into the "Crisper Basket".
8. Close the Ninja Foodi Grill with lid and set the time for 45 minutes.
9. Press "Start/Stop" to begin cooking.
10. When cooking time is completed, press "Start/Stop" to stop cooking and open the lid.
11. Place the roast onto a platter.
12. With a piece of foil, cover the roast for about 10 minutes before slicing.
13. Cut the roast into desired sized slices and serve.

Nutritional Information per Serving:

Calories: 362 | Fat: 14.2g | Saturated Fat: 4.7g | Carbohydrates: 0.3g | Sugar: 0g | Protein: 55.1g

49. Seasoned Beef Roast

⏰ Prep Time 10 m | ⏰ Cooking Time 45 m | 8 Servings

Ingredients:

- 2½ pounds beef roast
- 1 tablespoon olive oil
- 2 tablespoons Montreal steak seasoning

Instructions:

1. With kitchen twines, tie the roast into a compact shape.
2. Brush the roast with oil and then rub with seasoning.
3. Arrange the beef roast into a greased baking pan.
4. Arrange the "Crisper Basket" in the pot of Ninja Foodi Grill.
5. Close the Ninja Foodi Grill with lid and select "Air Crisp".
6. Set the temperature to 360 degrees F to preheat.
7. Press "Start/Stop" to begin preheating.
8. When the display shows "Add Food" open the lid and place the pan into the "Crisper Basket".
9. Close the Ninja Foodi Grill with lid and set the time for 45 minutes.
10. Press "Start/Stop" to begin cooking.
11. When the cooking time is completed, press "Start/Stop" to stop cooking and open the lid.
12. Place the steak onto a cutting board for about 10-15 minutes before slicing.
13. With a sharp knife, cut the steak into desired sized slices and serve.

Nutritional Information per Serving:

Calories: 283 | Fat: 10.6g | Saturated Fat: 3.6g | Carbohydrates: 0.9g | Sugar: 0g | Protein: 43g

50. Simple Beef Sirloin Roast

⏰ Prep Time 10 m | ⏰ Cooking Time 50 m | 8 Servings

Ingredients:

- 2½ pounds sirloin roast
- Salt and freshly ground black pepper, to taste

Instructions:

1. Rub the roast with salt and black pepper generously.
2. Arrange the "Crisper Basket" in the pot of Ninja Foodi Grill.
3. Close the Ninja Foodi Grill with lid and "Roast".
4. Set the temperature to 350 degrees F to preheat.
5. Press "Start/Stop" to begin preheating.
6. When the display shows "Add Food" open the lid and place the pan into the "Crisper Basket".
7. Close the Ninja Foodi Grill with lid and set the time for 50 minutes.
8. Press "Start/Stop" to begin cooking.
9. When the cooking time is completed, press "Start/Stop" to stop cooking and open the lid.
10. Place the steak onto a cutting board for about 10-15 minutes before slicing.
11. With a sharp knife, cut the steak into desired sized slices and serve.

Nutritional Information per Serving:
Calories: 201 | Fat: 8.8g | Saturated Fat: 3.1g | Carbohydrates: 0g | Sugar: 0g | Protein: 28.9g

51. Glazed Pork Ribs

⏰ Prep Time 15 m | ⏰ Cooking Time 13 m | 6 Servings

Ingredients:

- ¾ cup tomato sauce
- 3 tablespoons honey
- 1 tablespoon Worcestershire sauce
- 1 tablespoon low-sodium soy sauce
- 1 tablespoon fresh lime juice
- ½ teaspoon garlic powder
- ½ teaspoon red pepper flakes, crushed
- Freshly ground black pepper, to taste
- 2 pounds pork ribs

Instructions:

1. In a large bowl, add all the ingredients except pork ribs and mix well.
2. Add the pork ribs ad coat with the mixture generously.
3. Arrange the greased "Crisper Basket" in the pot of Ninja Foodi Grill.
4. Close the Ninja Foodi Grill with lid and select "Air Crisp".
5. Set the temperature to 355 degrees F to preheat.
6. Press "Start/Stop" to begin preheating.
7. When the display shows "Add Food" open the lid and place the pork ribs into the "Crisper Basket".
8. Close the Ninja Foodi Grill with lid and set the time for 13 minutes.
9. Press "Start/Stop" to begin cooking.
10. Flip the ribs once halfway through.
11. When cooking time is completed, press "Start/Stop" to stop cooking and open the lid.
12. Transfer the ribs onto a platter for about 5 minutes before serving.

Nutritional Information per Serving:
Calories: 457 | Fat: 26.9g | Saturated Fat: 9.5g | Carbohydrates: 11.3g | Sugar: 10.7g | Protein: 40.7g

52. Simple Pork Loin

⏰ Prep Time 10 m | ⏰ Cooking Time 30 m | 6 Servings

Ingredients:
- 2 pounds pork loin
- 2 tablespoons olive oil, divided
- Salt and freshly ground black pepper, to taste

Instructions:
1. Arrange a wire rack in a baking pan.
2. Coat the pork loin with oil and then, rub with salt and black pepper.
3. Arrange the pork loin into the prepared baking pan.
4. Arrange the "Crisper Basket" in the pot of Ninja Foodi Grill.
5. Close the Ninja Foodi Grill with lid and select "Bake"
6. Set the temperature to 350 degrees F to preheat.
7. Press "Start/Stop" to begin preheating.
8. When the display shows "Add Food" open the lid and place the pan into the "Crisper Basket".
9. Close the Ninja Foodi Grill with lid and set the time for 30 minutes.
10. Press "Start/Stop" to begin cooking.
11. When the cooking time is completed, press "Start/Stop" to stop cooking and open the lid.
12. Place the pork loin onto a cutting board.
13. With a piece of foil, cover the pork loin for about 10 minutes before slicing.
14. With a sharp knife, cut the pork loin into desired sized slices and serve.

Nutritional Information per Serving:
Calories: 406 | Fat: 25.7g | Saturated Fat: 8.6g | Carbohydrates: 0g | Sugar: 0g | Protein: 41.3g

53. Basil Pork Loin

⏰ Prep Time 10 m | ⏰ Cooking Time 20 m | 6 Servings

Ingredients:
- 3 tablespoons sugar
- 2 teaspoons dried basil
- 1 teaspoon garlic powder
- Salt, to taste
- 2 pounds pork loin

Instructions:
1. In a bowl, add the Sugar:, basil, garlic powder and salt and mix well.
2. Rub the pork loin with bail mixture generously.
3. Arrange the greased "Crisper Basket" in the pot of Ninja Foodi Grill.
4. Close the Ninja Foodi Grill with lid and select "Air Crisp".
5. Set the temperature to 400 degrees F to preheat.
6. Press "Start/Stop" to begin preheating.
7. When the display shows "Add Food" open the lid and place the pork loin into the "Crisper Basket".
8. Close the Ninja Foodi Grill with lid and set the time for 20 minutes.
9. Press "Start/Stop" to begin cooking.
10. Flip the pork loin once halfway through.
11. When the cooking time is completed, press "Start/Stop" to stop cooking and open the lid.
12. Place the pork loin onto a cutting board.
13. Cut the pork loin into desired sized slices and serve.

Nutritional Information per Serving:
Calories: 390 | Fat: 21.1g | Saturated Fat: 7.9g | Carbohydrates: 6.4g | Sugar: 6.1g | Protein: 41.4g

54. Glazed Pork Shoulder

⏰ Prep Time 15 m | ⏰ Cooking Time 8 m | 6 Servings

Ingredients:
- 1/3 cup soy sauce
- 2 tablespoons Sugar:
- 1 tablespoon honey
- 2 pounds pork shoulder, cut into 1½-inch thick slices

Instructions:
1. In a large bowl, place the soy sauce, Sugar:, and honey and mix well.
2. Add the pork slices and coat with marinade generously.
3. Cover the bowl and refrigerate to marinate for about 4-6 hours.
4. Arrange the greased "Crisper Basket" in the pot of Ninja Foodi Grill.
5. Close the Ninja Foodi Grill with lid and select "Air Crisp".
6. Set the temperature to 390 degrees F to preheat.
7. When the display shows "Add Food" open the lid and place the pork slices into the "Crisper Basket".
8. Close the Ninja Foodi Grill with lid and set the time for 8 minutes.
9. Press "Start/Stop" to begin cooking.
10. When the cooking time is completed, press "Start/Stop" to stop cooking and open the lid.
11. Serve hot.

Nutritional Information per Serving:
Calories: 475 | Fat: 32.4g | Saturated Fat: 11.9g | Carbohydrates: 8g | Sugar: 7.1g | Protein: 36.1g

55. Seasoned Pork Shoulder

⏰ Prep Time 15 m | ⏰ Cooking Time 1 h | 10 Servings

Ingredients:

- 3 pounds skin-on, bone-in pork shoulder
- 2-3 tablespoons adobo seasoning
- Salt, to taste

Instructions:

1. Arrange the pork shoulder onto a cutting board, skin-side down.
2. Season the inner side of pork shoulder with adobo seasoning and salt.
3. Season the inner side of pork shoulder with salt and adobo seasoning.
4. With kitchen twines, tie the pork shoulder into a long round cylinder shape.
5. Season the outer side of pork shoulder with salt.
6. Arrange the greased "Crisper Basket" in the pot of Ninja Foodi Grill.
7. Close the Ninja Foodi Grill with lid and select "Roast".
8. Set the temperature to 350 degrees F to preheat.
9. Press "Start/Stop" to begin preheating.
10. When the display shows "Add Food" open the lid and place the pork shoulder into the "Crisper Basket".
11. Close the Ninja Foodi Grill with lid and set the time for 60 minutes.
12. Press "Start/Stop" to begin cooking.
13. Flip the roast once halfway through.
14. When the cooking time is completed, press "Start/Stop" to stop cooking and open the lid.
15. Place onto a platter for about 10 minutes before slicing.
16. With a sharp knife, cut the pork shoulder into desired sized slices and serve.

Nutritional Information per Serving:
Calories: 397 | Fat: 29.1g | Saturated Fat: 10.7g | Carbohydrates: 0g | Sugar: 0g | Protein: 31.7g

56. Stuffed Pork Roll

⏰ Prep Time 20 m | ⏰ Cooking Time 15 m | 4 Servings

Ingredients:

- 1 scallion, chopped
- ¼ cup sun-dried tomatoes, chopped finely
- 2 tablespoons fresh parsley, chopped
- Salt and freshly ground black pepper, to taste
- 4 (6-ounce) pork cutlets, pounded slightly
- 2 teaspoons paprika
- ½ tablespoons olive oil

Instructions:

1. In a bowl, mix together the scallion, tomatoes, parsley, salt, and black pepper.
2. Spread the tomato mixture over each pork cutlet.
3. Roll each cutlet and secure with cocktail sticks.
4. Rub the outer part of rolls with paprika, salt and black pepper.
5. Coat the rolls with oil evenly.
6. Arrange the greased "Crisper Basket" in the pot of Ninja Foodi Grill.
7. Close the Ninja Foodi Grill with lid and select "Air Crisp".
8. Set the temperature to 390 degrees F to preheat.
9. Press "Start/Stop" to begin preheating.
10. When the display shows "Add Food" open the lid and place the pork rolls into the "Crisper Basket" in a single layer.
11. Close the Ninja Foodi Grill with lid and set the time for 15 minutes.
12. Press "Start/Stop" to begin cooking.
13. When the cooking time is completed, press "Start/Stop" to stop cooking and open the lid.
14. Serve hot.

Nutritional Information per Serving:
Calories: 244 | Fat: 14.5g | Saturated Fat: 2.7g | Carbohydrates: 20.1g | Sugar: 1.7g | Protein: 8.2g

57. Glazed Pork Tenderloin

⏰ Prep Time 15 m | ⏰ Cooking Time 20 m | 3 Servings

Ingredients:

- 2 tablespoons red hot sauce
- 2 tablespoons honey
- 1 tablespoon fresh rosemary, minced
- ¼ teaspoon red pepper flakes, crushed
- Salt, to taste
- 1 pound pork tenderloin

Instructions:

1. In a small bowl, add the hot sauce, honey, rosemary, red pepper flakes and salt and mix well.
2. Brush the pork tenderloin with mixture evenly.
3. Arrange the greased "Crisper Basket" in the pot of Ninja Foodi Grill.
4. Close the Ninja Foodi Grill with lid and select "Air Crisp".
5. Set the temperature to 350 degrees F to preheat.
6. Press "Start/Stop" to begin preheating.
7. When the display shows "Add Food" open the lid and place the pork tenderloin into the "Crisper Basket".
8. Close the Ninja Foodi Grill with lid and set the time for 20 minutes.
9. Press "Start/Stop" to begin cooking.
10. When the cooking time is completed, press "Start/Stop" to stop cooking and open the lid.
11. Place the pork tenderloin onto a cutting board for about 10 minutes before slicing.
12. With a sharp knife, cut the tenderloin into desired sized slices and serve.

Nutritional Information per Serving:

Calories: 264 | Fat: 5.6g | Saturated Fat: 1.9g | Carbohydrates: 12.5g | Sugar: 11.6g | Protein: 39.7g

58. Bacon-Wrapped Pork Tenderloin

⏰ Prep Time 15 m | ⏰ Cooking Time 30 m | 4 Servings

Ingredients:
- 1 (1½-pound) pork tenderloin
- 2 tablespoons Dijon mustard
- 1 tablespoon honey
- 4 bacon strips

Instructions:
1. Coat the tenderloin with mustard and honey.
2. Wrap the pork tenderloin with bacon strips.
3. Place the pork loin into a greased air fryer basket.
4. Arrange the greased "Crisper Basket" in the pot of Ninja Foodi Grill.
5. Close the Ninja Foodi Grill with lid and select "Air Crisp".
6. Set the temperature to 360 degrees F to preheat.
7. Press "Start/Stop" to begin preheating.
8. When the display shows "Add Food" open the lid and place the pork tenderloin into the "Crisper Basket".
9. Close the Ninja Foodi Grill with lid and set the time for 30 minutes.
10. Press "Start/Stop" to begin cooking.
11. Flip the tenderloin once halfway through.
12. When the cooking time is completed, press "Start/Stop" to stop cooking and open the lid.
13. Place the pork tenderloin onto a cutting board for about 10 minutes before slicing.
14. With a sharp knife, cut the tenderloin into desired sized slices and serve.

Nutritional Information per Serving:
Calories: 386 | Fat: 16.1g | Saturated Fat: 5.7g | Carbohydrates: 4.8g | Sugar: 4.4g | Protein: 52.6g

59. Pork Loin with Potatoes

⏰ Prep Time 15 m | ⏰ Cooking Time 25 m | 6 Servings

Ingredients:

- 2 pounds pork loin
- 3 tablespoons olive oil, divided
- 1 teaspoon fresh parsley, chopped
- Salt and freshly ground black pepper, to taste
- 3 large red potatoes, chopped
- ½ teaspoon garlic powder
- ½ teaspoon red pepper flakes, crushed

Instructions:

1. Coat the pork loin with oil and then season with parsley salt, and black pepper.
2. In a large bowl, add the potatoes, remaining oil, garlic powder, red pepper flakes, salt, and black pepper and toss to coat well.
3. Arrange the greased "Crisper Basket" in the pot of Ninja Foodi Grill.
4. Close the Ninja Foodi Grill with lid and select
5. Set the temperature to 325 degrees F to preheat.
6. Press "Start/Stop" to begin preheating.
7. When the display shows "Add Food" open the lid and place the pork loin into the "Crisper Basket".
8. Arrange potato pieces around the pork loin.
9. Close the Ninja Foodi Grill with lid and set the time for 25 minutes.
10. Press "Start/Stop" to begin cooking.
11. When the cooking time is completed, press "Start/Stop" to stop cooking and open the lid.
12. Place the pork loin onto a platter for about 5 minutes before slicing.
13. Cut the pork loin into desired size slices and serve alongside the potatoes.

Nutritional Information per Serving:

Calories: 556 | Fat: 28.g | Saturated Fat: 9g | Carbohydrates: 29.6g | Sugar: 1.9g | Protein: 44.9g

60. Pork Taco Casserole

⏰ Prep Time 10 m | ⏰ Cooking Time 25 m | 6 Servings

Ingredients:

- 2 pounds ground pork
- 2 tablespoons taco seasoning
- 1 cup cheddar cheese, shredded
- 1 cup cottage cheese
- 1 cup salsa

Instructions:

1. In a bowl, add the pork and taco seasoning and mix well.
2. Add the cheeses and salsa and stir to combine.
3. Place the mixture into the baking pan.
4. Arrange the "Crisper Basket" in the pot of Ninja Foodi Grill.
5. Close the Ninja Foodi Grill with lid and select "Air Crisp".
6. Set the temperature to 375 degrees F to preheat.
7. Press "Start/Stop" to begin preheating.
8. When the display shows "Add Food" open the lid and place the pan into the "Crisper Basket".
9. Close the Ninja Foodi Grill with lid and set the time for 25 minutes.
10. Press "Start/Stop" to begin cooking.
11. When the cooking time is completed, press "Start/Stop" to stop cooking and open the lid.
12. Set the baking pan aside for about 5 minutes before serving.
13. Divide the casserole into desired sized pieces and serve.

Nutritional Information per Serving:

Calories: 412 | Fat: 16.5g | Saturated Fat: 8g | Carbohydrates: 6.3 g | Sugar: 2.1 g | Protein: 56.4 g

61. Sausage Casserole

⏰ Prep Time 15 m | ⏰ Cooking Time 30 m | 4 Servings

Ingredients:

- 6 ounces flour, sifted
- 2 eggs
- 1 red onion, thinly sliced
- 1 garlic clove, minced
- Salt and freshly ground black pepper, to taste
- ¾ cup milk
- 2/3 cup cold water
- 8 small sausages
- 8 fresh rosemary sprigs

Instructions:

1. In a bowl, mix together the flour and eggs.
2. Slowly add in the milk and water and mix until well combined.
3. In each sausage, pierce 1 rosemary sprig.
4. Arrange sausages into a greased baking pan and top evenly with the flour mixture.
5. Arrange the "Crisper Basket" in the pot of Ninja Foodi Grill.
6. Close the Ninja Foodi Grill with lid and select "Air Crisp".
7. Set the temperature to 320 degrees F to preheat.
8. Press "Start/Stop" to begin preheating.
9. When the display shows "Add Food" open the lid and place the pan into the "Crisper Basket".
10. Close the Ninja Foodi Grill with lid and set the time for 30 minutes.
11. Press "Start/Stop" to begin cooking.
12. When the cooking time is completed, press "Start/Stop" to stop cooking and open the lid.
13. Serve warm.

Nutritional Information per Serving:

Calories: 730 | Fat: 46.1g | Saturated Fat: 15g | Carbohydrates: 37.7g | Sugar: 3.5g | Protein: 38.2g

62. Glazed Ham

⏰ Prep Time 15 m | ⏰ Cooking Time 40 m | 4 Servings

Ingredients:
- 1 pound 10½ ounces ham
- 1 cup whiskey
- 2 tablespoons French mustard
- 2 tablespoons honey

Instructions:
1. Place the ham at room temperature for about 30 minutes before cooking.
2. In a bowl, mix together the whiskey, mustard and honey.
3. Place the ham in a baking pan.
4. Top with half of the honey mixture and coat well.
5. Arrange the "Crisper Basket" in the pot of Ninja Foodi Grill
6. Close the Ninja Foodi Grill with lid and select "Air Crisp".
7. Set the temperature to 320 degrees F to preheat.
8. Press "Start/Stop" to begin preheating.
9. When the display shows "Add Food" open the lid and place the pan into the "Crisper Basket".
10. Close the Ninja Foodi Grill with lid and set the time for 40 minutes.
11. Press "Start/Stop" to begin cooking.
12. After 15 minutes of cooking, flip the side of ham and top with the remaining honey mixture.
13. When cooking time is completed, press "Start/Stop" to stop cooking and open the lid.
14. Place the ham onto a platter for about 10 minutes before slicing.
15. Cut the ham into desired sized slices and serve.

Nutritional Information per Serving:
Calories: 477 | Fat: 16.2g | Saturated Fat: 5.5g | Carbohydrates: 15.9g | Sugar: 8.7g | Protein: 31.2g

63. Marinated Lamb Chops

⏰ Prep Time 15 m | ⏰ Cooking Time 17 m | 8 Servings

Ingredients:

- 2 teaspoons Dijon mustard
- 2 teaspoons olive oil
- 1 teaspoon soy sauce
- 1 teaspoon garlic, minced
- 1 teaspoon ground cumin
- 1 teaspoon cayenne pepper
- 8 (6-ounce) lamb chops

Instructions:

1. For marinade: in a bowl, place all ingredients except for chops and mix well.
2. Add the chops and coat with marinade generously.
3. Refrigerate to marinate for at least 30 minutes, up to overnight.
4. Arrange the greased "Crisper Basket" in the pot of Ninja Foodi Grill.
5. Close the Ninja Foodi Grill with lid and select "Air Crisp".
6. Set the temperature to 350 degrees F to preheat.
7. Press "Start/Stop" to begin preheating.
8. When the display shows "Add Food" open the lid and place the lamb chops into the "Crisper Basket".
9. Close the Ninja Foodi Grill with lid and set the time for 17 minutes.
10. Press "Start/Stop" to begin cooking.
11. Flip the chops once halfway through.
12. When the cooking time is completed, press "Start/Stop" to stop cooking and open the lid.
13. Serve hot

Nutritional Information per Serving:

Calories: 330 | Fat: 13.8g | Saturated Fat: 4.6g | Carbohydrates: 0.5g | Sugar: 0.1g | Protein: 48g

64. Lamb Chops with Veggies

Prep Time 15 m | Cooking Time 8 m | 4 Servings

Ingredients:

- 2 tablespoons fresh rosemary, minced
- 2 tablespoons fresh mint leaves, minced
- 1 garlic clove, minced
- 3 tablespoons olive oil
- Salt and freshly ground black pepper, to taste
- 4 (6-ounce) lamb chops
- 1 purple carrot, peeled and cubed
- 1 yellow carrot, peeled and cubed
- 1 parsnip, peeled and cubed
- 1 fennel bulb, cubed

Instructions:

1. In a large bowl, mix together the herbs, garlic, oil, salt, and black pepper.
2. Add the chops and generously coat with mixture.
3. Refrigerate to marinate for about 3 hours.
4. In a large pan of water, soak the vegetables for about 15 minutes.
5. Drain the vegetables completely.
6. Arrange the greased "Crisper Basket" in the pot of Ninja Foodi Grill.
7. Close the Ninja Foodi Grill with lid and select "Air Crisp".
8. Set the temperature to 390 degrees F to preheat.
9. Press "Start/Stop" to begin preheating.
10. When the display shows "Add Food" open the lid and place the lamb chops into the "Crisper Basket".
11. Close the Ninja Foodi Grill with lid and set the time for 2 minutes.
12. Press "Start/Stop" to begin cooking.
13. When the cooking time is completed, press "Start/Stop" to stop cooking and open the lid.
14. Transfer the chops onto a platter and top with the remaining garlic mixture.
15. Serve hot
16. Remove chops from "Crisper Basket".
17. Arrange the vegetables into the "Crisper Basket" and top with the chops in a single layer.
18. Close the Ninja Foodi Grill with lid and set the time for 6 minutes.
19. Press "Start/Stop" to begin cooking.
20. When the cooking time is completed, press "Start/Stop" to stop cooking and open the lid.
21. Transfer the chops and vegetables onto serving plates and serve.

Nutritional Information per Serving:

Calories: 467 | Fat: 23.5g | Saturated Fat: 6.1g | Carbohydrates: 14.2g | Sugar: 3g | Protein: 49.3g

65. Herbed Rack of Lamb

⏰ Prep Time 10 m | ⏰ Cooking Time 15 m | 6 Servings

Ingredients:
- 4 tablespoons olive oil
- 2 tablespoons dried rosemary
- 1 tablespoon dried thyme
- 2 teaspoons garlic, minced
- Salt and freshly ground black pepper, to taste
- 2 pounds rack of lamb

Instructions:
1. in a small bowl, mix together the oil, herbs, garlic, salt and black pepper and mix well.
2. Add the rack of lamb and coat with mixture generously.
3. Arrange the "Crisper Basket" in the pot of Ninja Foodi Grill.
4. Close the Ninja Foodi Grill with lid and select "Air Crisp".
5. Set the temperature to 380 degrees F to preheat.
6. Press "Start/Stop" to begin preheating.
7. When the display shows "Add Food" open the lid and place the rack of lamb into the "Crisper Basket".
8. Close the Ninja Foodi Grill with lid and set the time for 10 minutes.
9. Press "Start/Stop" to begin cooking.
10. When the cooking time is completed, press "Start/Stop" to stop cooking and open the lid.
11. Place the rack of lamb onto a cutting board for about 10 minutes.
12. Cut the rack into individual chops and serve.

Nutritional Information per Serving:
Calories: 341 | Fat: 22.9g | Saturated Fat: 6.1g | Carbohydrates: 1.3g | Sugar: 0g | Protein: 30.9g

66. Almond Crusted Rack of Lamb

⏰ Prep Time 15 m | ⏰ Cooking Time 35 m | 6 Servings

Ingredients:

- 1 (1¾-pound) rack of lamb
- Salt and freshly ground black pepper, to taste
- Olive oil cooking spray
- 1 egg
- 1 tablespoon breadcrumbs
- 3 ounces almonds, chopped finely

Instructions:

1. Season the rack of lamb with salt and black pepper evenly and then spray with cooking spray.
2. In a shallow dish, beat the egg.
3. In another shallow dish, mix together the breadcrumbs and almonds.
4. Dip the rack of lamb in egg and then coat with the almond mixture.
5. Arrange the greased "Crisper Basket" in the pot of Ninja Foodi Grill.
6. Close the Ninja Foodi Grill with lid and select "Air Crisp".
7. Set the temperature to 220 degrees F to preheat.
8. Press "Start/Stop" to begin preheating.
9. When the display shows "Add Food" open the lid and place the rack of lamb into the "Crisper Basket".
10. Close the Ninja Foodi Grill with lid and set the time for 30 minutes.
11. Press "Start/Stop" to begin cooking.
12. After 30 minutes of cooking, set the temperature to 390 degrees F for 5 minutes.
13. When the cooking time is completed, press "Start/Stop" to stop cooking and open the lid.
14. Place the rack of lamb onto a cutting board for about 10 minutes.
15. Cut the rack into individual chops and serve.

Nutritional Information per Serving:

Calories: 319 | Fat: 19.6g | Saturated Fat: 4.9g | Carbohydrates: 3.9g | Sugar: 0.7g | Protein: 31g

67. Pesto Rack of Lamb

⏰ Prep Time 15 m | ⏰ Cooking Time 15 m | 4 Servings

Ingredients:
- ½ bunch fresh mint
- 1 garlic clove
- ¼ cup extra-virgin olive oil
- ½ tablespoons honey
- Salt and freshly ground black pepper, to taste
- 1 (1½-pound) rack of lamb

Instructions:
1. For pesto: in a blender, add the mint, garlic, oil, honey, salt, and black pepper and pulse until smooth.
2. Coat the rack of lamb with some pesto evenly.
3. Arrange the greased "Crisper Basket" in the pot of Ninja Foodi Grill.
4. Close the Ninja Foodi Grill with lid and select "Air Crisp".
5. Set the temperature to 200 degrees F to preheat.
6. Press "Start/Stop" to begin preheating.
7. When the display shows "Add Food" open the lid and place the rack of lamb into the "Crisper Basket".
8. Close the Ninja Foodi Grill with lid and set the time for 15 minutes.
9. Press "Start/Stop" to begin cooking.
10. While cooking, coat the rack of lamb with the remaining pesto after every 5 minutes.
11. When the cooking time is completed, press "Start/Stop" to stop cooking and open the lid.
12. Place the rack of lamb onto a cutting board for about 10 minutes.
13. Cut the rack into individual chops and serve.

Nutritional Information per Serving:
Calories: 405 | Fat: 27.7g | Saturated Fat: 7.1g | Carbohydrates: 2.8g | Sugar: 2.2g | Protein: 34.8g

68. Parmesan Crusted Rack of Lamb

⏰ Prep Time 15 m | ⏰ Cooking Time 18 m | 4 Servings

Ingredients:

- 1 (1½-pound) rack of lamb, frenched
- 3 tablespoons extra-virgin olive oil
- Salt and freshly ground black pepper, to taste
- ½ cup Parmesan cheese, grated
- 1/3 cup panko breadcrumbs
- 1 large garlic clove, grated
- 1 teaspoon fresh thyme, chopped finely
- 1 teaspoon fresh rosemary, chopped finely
- Nonstick cooking spray

Instructions:

1. Rub the rack of lamb with 1 tablespoon of the olive oil and then season with salt and black pepper.
2. In a shallow bowl, add the Parmesan, panko, remaining 2 tablespoons olive oil, grated garlic and herbs and mix well.
3. Add the lamb and coat with the Parmesan mixture evenly.
4. Arrange the greased "Crisper Basket" in the pot of Ninja Foodi Grill.
5. Close the Ninja Foodi Grill with lid and select "Air Crisp".
6. Set the temperature to 375 degrees F to preheat.
7. Press "Start/Stop" to begin preheating.
8. When the display shows "Add Food" open the lid and place the rack of lamb into the "Crisper Basket".
9. Spray the rack of lamb with cooking spray.
10. Close the Ninja Foodi Grill with lid and set the time for 18 minutes.
11. Press "Start/Stop" to begin cooking.
12. When the cooking time is completed, press "Start/Stop" to stop cooking and open the lid.
13. Place the rack of lamb onto a cutting board for about 10 minutes.
14. Cut the rack into individual chops and serve.

Nutritional Information per Serving:

Calories: 657 | Fat: 54.2g | Saturated Fat: 24.1g | Carbohydrates: 1.7g | Sugar: 0g | Protein: 32.9g

69. Garlicky Lamb Steaks

⏰ Prep Time 15 m | ⏰ Cooking Time 15 m | 4 Servings

Ingredients:

- ½ onion, roughly chopped
- 5 garlic cloves, peeled
- 1 tablespoon fresh ginger, peeled
- 1 teaspoon ground fennel
- ½ teaspoon ground cumin
- ½ teaspoon ground cinnamon
- ½ teaspoon cayenne pepper
- Salt and freshly ground black pepper, to taste
- 1½ pounds boneless lamb sirloin steaks

Instructions:

1. In a blender, add the onion, garlic, ginger, and spices and pulse until smooth.
2. Transfer the mixture into a large bowl.
3. Add the lamb steaks and coat with the mixture generously.
4. Refrigerate to marinate for about 24 hours.
5. Arrange the "Crisper Basket" in the pot of Ninja Foodi Grill.
6. Close the Ninja Foodi Grill with lid and select "Air Crisp".
7. Set the temperature to 330 degrees F to preheat.
8. Press "Start/Stop" to begin preheating.
9. When the display shows "Add Food" open the lid and place the lamb steaks into the "Crisper Basket".
10. Close the Ninja Foodi Grill with lid and set the time for 15 minutes.
11. Press "Start/Stop" to begin cooking.
12. When the cooking time is completed, press "Start/Stop" to stop cooking and open the lid.
13. Serve hot.

Nutritional Information per Serving:
Calories: 336 | Fat: 12.8g | Saturated Fat: 4.5g | Carbohydrates: 4.2g | Sugar: 0.7g | Protein: 48.4g

70. Lamb Rump with Carrots

⏰ Prep Time 15 m | ⏰ Cooking Time 35 m | 4 Servings

Ingredients:

- 1 pound 5 ounces lamb rump
- 2 garlic clove, crushed
- 1 tablespoon dried rosemary, crushed
- 2 large carrots, peeled and cubed
- ½ of large yellow onion, peeled and halved
- 2 teaspoons olive oil

Instructions:

1. Rub the lamb with crushed garlic evenly and sprinkle with rosemary evenly.
2. Arrange the greased "Crisper Basket" in the pot of Ninja Foodi Grill.
3. Close the Ninja Foodi Grill with lid and select "Air Crisp".
4. Set the temperature to 355 degrees F to preheat.
5. Press "Start/Stop" to begin preheating.
6. When the display shows "Add Food" open the lid and place the lamb rump into the "Crisper Basket".
7. Close the Ninja Foodi Grill with lid and set the time for 20 minutes.
8. Press "Start/Stop" to begin cooking.
9. Meanwhile, in a large bowl, add carrots, onions and oil and toss to coat well.
10. After 20 minutes of cooking, place the carrot mixture on top of the lamb rump.
11. Close the Ninja Foodi Grill with lid and set the temperature to 390 degrees F for 15 minutes.
12. When the cooking time is completed, press "Start/Stop" to stop cooking and open the lid.
13. Serve hot.

Nutritional Information per Serving:
Calories: 293 | Fat: 16.2g | Saturated Fat: 0 g | Carbohydrates: 5.1g | Sugar: 2.1g | Protein: 30.3g

71. Glazed Leg of Lamb

⏰ Prep Time 15 m | ⏰ Cooking Time 1 h 40 m | 10 Servings

Ingredients:

- ¼ cup olive oil
- 4 garlic cloves, chopped
- ¼ cup fresh rosemary
- 3 tablespoons Dijon mustard
- 2 tablespoons maple syrup
- Salt and freshly ground black pepper, to taste
- 1 (4-pound) leg of lamb

Instructions:

1. In a food processor, add the oil, garlic, herbs, mustard, honey, salt and black pepper and pulse until smooth.
2. Place the leg of lamb and marinade into a glass baking pan and mix well
3. With plastic wrap, cover the baking pan and refrigerate to marinate for 6-8 hours.
4. Arrange a wire rack in a baking pan.
5. Arrange the leg of lamb into the prepared baking pan.
6. Arrange the "Crisper Basket" in the pot of Ninja Foodi Grill.
7. Close the Ninja Foodi Grill with lid and select "Bake".
8. Set the temperature to 420 degrees F to preheat.
9. Press "Start/Stop" to begin preheating.
10. When the display shows "Add Food" open the lid and place the pan into the "Crisper Basket".
11. Close the Ninja Foodi Grill with lid and set the time for 20 minutes.
12. Press "Start/Stop" to begin cooking.
13. After 20 minutes of cooking, set the temperature to 320 degrees F for 80 minutes.
14. When the cooking time is completed, press "Start/Stop" to stop cooking and open the lid.
15. Place the leg of lamb onto a cutting board.
16. With a piece of foil, cover the leg of lamb for about 10 minutes before slicing.
17. With a sharp knife, cut the leg of lamb into desired sized slices and serve.

Nutritional Information per Serving:
Calories: 401 | Fat: 18.8g | Saturated Fat: 5.6g | Carbohydrates: 4.3g | Sugar: 2.4g | Protein: 51.3g

72. Garlicky Lamb Roast

⏰ Prep Time 15 m | ⏰ Cooking Time 1 h 30 m | 8 Servings

Ingredients:

- 2¾ pounds lamb leg roast
- 3 garlic cloves, cut into thin slices
- 2 tablespoons extra-virgin olive oil
- 1 tablespoon dried rosemary, crushed
- Salt and freshly ground black pepper, to taste

Instructions:

1. In a small bowl, mix together the oil, rosemary, salt, and black pepper.
2. With the tip of a sharp knife, make deep slits on the top of lamb roast fat.
3. Insert the garlic slices into the slits.
4. Coat the lamb roast with oil mixture evenly.
5. Arrange the "Crisper Basket" in the pot of Ninja Foodi Grill.
6. Close the Ninja Foodi Grill with lid and select "Air Crisp".
7. Set the temperature to 390 degrees F to preheat.
8. Press "Start/Stop" to begin preheating.
9. When the display shows "Add Food" open the lid and place the lamb roast into the "Crisper Basket".
10. Close the Ninja Foodi Grill with lid and set the time for 15 minutes.
11. Press "Start/Stop" to begin cooking.
12. After 15 minutes of cooking, set the temperature to 320 degrees F for 75 minutes.
13. When the cooking time is completed, press "Start/Stop" to stop cooking and open the lid.
14. Place the roast onto a platter.
15. With a piece of foil, cover the roast for about 10 minutes before slicing.
16. Cut the roast into desired sized slices and serve.

Nutritional Information per Serving:
Calories: 314 | Fat: 14g | Saturated Fat: 4.2g | Carbohydrates: 0.6g | Sugar: 0g | Protein: 44g

73. Lamb Meatloaf

⏰ Prep Time 15 m | ⏰ Cooking Time 20 m | 4 Servings

Ingredients:

- 1 pound ground lamb
- 1 cup fresh kale leaves, trimmed and finely chopped
- 1 cup onion, chopped
- 1 (4-ounces) can diced green chilies
- 2 garlic cloves, minced
- 1 egg, beaten
- ½ cup fresh breadcrumbs
- 1 cup Monterey Jack cheese, grated
- ¼ cup salsa verde
- 3 tablespoons fresh cilantro, chopped
- 1 teaspoon red chili powder
- ½ teaspoon ground cumin
- ½ teaspoon dried oregano, crushed
- Salt and freshly ground black pepper, to taste

Instructions:

1. In a shallow bowl, place all the ingredients and with your hands, mix until well combined.
2. Divide the turkey mixture into 4 equal-sized portions and shape each into a mini loaf.
3. Arrange the greased "Crisper Basket" in the pot of Ninja Foodi Grill.
4. Close the Ninja Foodi Grill with lid and select "Air Crisp".
5. Set the temperature to 400 degrees F to preheat.
6. Press "Start/Stop" to begin preheating.
7. When the display shows "Add Food" open the lid and place the loaves into the "Crisper Basket".
8. Close the Ninja Foodi Grill with lid and set the time for 20 minutes.
9. Press "Start/Stop" to begin cooking.
10. When the cooking time is completed, press "Start/Stop" to stop cooking and open the lid.
11. Place the loaves onto plates for about 5 minutes before serving.

Nutritional Information per Serving:

Calories: 507 | Fat: 20.6g | Saturated Fat: 9.1g | Carbohydrates: 36g | Sugar: 1.3g | Protein: 46.2g

74. Lamb Stuffed Bell Peppers

⏰ Prep Time 15 m | ⏰ Cooking Time 25 m | 6 Servings

Ingredients:

- 6 green bell peppers
- 1¼ pounds lean ground lamb
- 1 cup marinara sauce
- 1/3 cup scallion, chopped
- ¼ cup fresh parsley, chopped
- ½ teaspoon dried sage, crushed
- ½ teaspoon garlic salt
- 1 tablespoon olive oil
- ¼ cup mozzarella cheese, shredded

Instructions:

1. Cut the top off of each bell pepper and carefully remove the seeds. Set aside.
2. Heat a nonstick skillet over medium-high heat and cook the ground lamb for about 8-10 minutes.
3. Drain the grease completely.
4. Add the marinara sauce, scallion, parsley, sage, salt and oil and mix well.
5. Stuff each bell pepper with lamb mixture.
6. Arrange the greased "Crisper Basket" in the pot of Ninja Foodi Grill.
7. Close the Ninja Foodi Grill with lid and select "Air Crisp".
8. Set the temperature to 355 degrees F to preheat.
9. Press "Start/Stop" to begin preheating.
10. When the display shows "Add Food" open the lid and place the bell peppers into the "Crisper Basket".
11. Close the Ninja Foodi Grill with lid and set the time for 25 minutes.
12. Press "Start/Stop" to begin cooking.
13. After 10 minutes of cooking, top each bell pepper with cheese.
14. When cooking time is completed, press "Start/Stop" to stop cooking and open the lid.
15. Serve hot.

Nutritional Information per Serving:

Calories: 207 | Fat: 10.7g | Saturated Fat: 3.2g | Carbohydrates: 15.6g | Sugar: 9.9g | Protein: 29g

75. Spicy Lamb Burgers

⏲ Prep Time 15 m | ⏲ Cooking Time 10 m | 6 Servings

Ingredients:

- 2 pounds ground lamb
- ½ tablespoon garlic powder
- ¼ teaspoon ground cumin
- ¼ teaspoon cayenne pepper
- Salt and freshly ground black pepper, to taste

Instructions:

1. In a bowl, add all the ingredients and mix well.
2. Make 6 equal-sized patties from the mixture.
3. Arrange the patties onto the greased baking pan in a single layer.
4. Arrange the "Crisper Basket" in the pot of Ninja Foodi Grill.
5. Close the Ninja Foodi Grill with lid and select "Air Crisp".
6. Set the temperature to 360 degrees F to preheat.
7. Press "Start/Stop" to begin preheating.
8. When the display shows "Add Food" open the lid and place the pan into the "Crisper Basket".
9. Close the Ninja Foodi Grill with lid and set the time for 10 minutes.
10. Press "Start/Stop" to begin cooking.
11. Flip the burgers once halfway through.
12. When the cooking time is completed, press "Start/Stop" to stop cooking and open the lid.
13. Serve hot.

Nutritional Information per Serving:

Calories: 284 | Fat: 11.1g | Saturated Fat: 5 g | Carbohydrates: 0.6g | Sugar: 0.2g | Protein 27 g

FISH & SEAFOOD RECIPES

76. Simple Salmon

⏰ Prep Time 10 m | ⏰ Cooking Time 12 m | 4 Servings

Ingredients:

- 4 (6-ounce) salmon fillets
- Salt and freshly ground black pepper, to taste

Instructions:

1. Season the salmon fillets with salt and black pepper evenly.
2. Arrange the "Grill Grate" in the pot of Ninja Foodi Grill.
3. Close the Ninja Foodi Grill with lid and select "Grill" on "Medium" to preheat.
4. Press "Start/Stop" to begin preheating.
5. When the display shows "Add Food" open the lid and place the fillets onto the "Grill Grate".
6. With your hands, gently press down each fillet slightly.
7. Close the Ninja Foodi Grill with lid and set the time for 12 minutes.
8. Press "Start/Stop" to begin cooking.
9. Flip the fillets once halfway through.
10. When the cooking time is completed, press "Start/Stop" to stop cooking and open the lid.
11. Serve hot.

Nutritional Information per Serving:

Calories: 225 | Fat: 10.5g | Saturated Fat: 1.5g | Carbohydrates: 0g | Sugar: 0g | Protein: 33g

77. Buttered Salmon

⏰ Prep Time 10 m | ⏰ Cooking Time 10 m | 2 Servings

Ingredients:

- 2 (6-ounce) salmon fillets
- Salt and freshly ground black pepper, to taste
- ¼ teaspoon dried rosemary, crushed
- 1 tablespoon butter, melted

Instructions:

1. Season each salmon fillet with salt and black pepper and then sprinkle with rosemary evenly.
2. Now, coat each fillet with the melted butter.
3. Arrange the greased "Crisper Basket" in the pot of Ninja Foodi Grill.
4. Close the Ninja Foodi Grill with lid and select "Air Crisp".
5. Set the temperature to 360 degrees F to preheat.
6. Press "Start/Stop" to begin preheating.
7. When the display shows "Add Food" open the lid and place the fillets into the "Crisper Basket".
8. Close the Ninja Foodi Grill with lid and set the time for 10 minutes.
9. Press "Start/Stop" to begin cooking.
10. When the cooking time is completed, press "Start/Stop" to stop cooking and open the lid.
11. Serve hot.

Nutritional Information per Serving:

Calories: 276 | Fat: 16.3g | Saturated Fat: 5.2g | Carbohydrates: 0g | Sugar: 0g | Protein: 33.1g

78. Zesty Salmon

⏰ Prep Time 10 m | ⏰ Cooking Time 8 m | 4 Servings

Ingredients:

- 1½ pounds salmon fillets
- ½ teaspoon red chili powder
- Salt and freshly ground black pepper, to taste
- 1 lime, cut into slices
- 1 tablespoon fresh dill, chopped

Instructions:

1. Season the salmon with chili powder, salt, and black pepper evenly.
2. Arrange the greased "Crisper Basket" in the pot of Ninja Foodi Grill.
3. Close the Ninja Foodi Grill with lid and select "Air Crisp".
4. Set the temperature to 375 degrees F to preheat.
5. Press "Start/Stop" to begin preheating.
6. When the display shows "Add Food" open the lid and place the fillets into the "Crisper Basket".
7. Close the Ninja Foodi Grill with lid and set the time for 8 minutes.
8. Press "Start/Stop" to begin cooking.
9. When the cooking time is completed, press "Start/Stop" to stop cooking and open the lid.
10. Serve hot with the garnishing of dill.

Nutritional Information per Serving:

Calories: 229 | Fat: 10.6g | Saturated Fat: 1.5g | Carbohydrates: 1g | Sugar: 0.1g | Protein: 33.2g

79. Cajun Salmon

⏰ Prep Time 10 m | ⏰ Cooking Time 8 m | 2 Servings

Ingredients:

- 2 (6-ounce) salmon steaks
- 2 tablespoons Cajun seasoning

Instructions:

1. Rub the salmon steaks with the Cajun seasoning evenly and set aside for about 10 minutes.
2. Arrange the "Crisper Basket" in the pot of Ninja Foodi Grill.
3. Close the Ninja Foodi Grill with lid and select "Air Crisp".
4. Set the temperature to 390 degrees F to preheat.
5. Press "Start/Stop" to begin preheating.
6. When the display shows "Add Food" open the lid and place the salmon steaks into the "Crisper Basket".
7. Close the Ninja Foodi Grill with lid and set the time for 8 minutes.
8. Press "Start/Stop" to begin cooking.
9. When the cooking time is completed, press "Start/Stop" to stop cooking and open the lid.
10. Serve hot.

Nutritional Information per Serving:

Calories: 225 | Fat: 10.5g | Saturated Fat: 1.5g | Carbohydrates: 0g | Sugar: 0g | Protein: 22.1g

80. Teriyaki Salmon

⏰ Prep Time 10 m | ⏰ Cooking Time 8 m | 4 Servings

Ingredients:
- 4 (6-ounce) skinless salmon fillets
- 1 cup teriyaki marinade

Instructions:
1. In a bowl, place all the salmon fillets and teriyaki marinade and mix well.
2. Refrigerate, covered to marinate for about 2-3 hours.
3. Arrange the "Grill Grate" in the pot of Ninja Foodi Grill.
4. Close the Ninja Foodi Grill with lid and select "Grill" to "Max" to preheat.
5. Press "Start/Stop" to begin preheating.
6. When the display shows "Add Food" open the lid and place the salmon fillets onto the "Grill Grate".
7. With your hands, gently press down salmon fillet.
8. Close the Ninja Foodi Grill with lid and set the time for 8 minutes.
9. Press "Start/Stop" to begin cooking.
10. After 6 minutes of cooking, flip the salmon fillets.
11. When the cooking time is completed, press "Start/Stop" to stop cooking and open the lid.
12. Serve hot.

Nutritional Information per Serving:
Calories: 305 | Fat: 10.5g | Saturated Fat: 1.5g | Carbohydrates: 16g | Sugar: 12g | Protein: 33g

81. Buttered Halibut

⏰ Prep Time 10 m | ⏰ Cooking Time 30 m | 4 Servings

Ingredients:
- 1 pound halibut fillets
- 1 tablespoon ginger paste
- 1 tablespoon garlic paste
- Salt and freshly ground black pepper, to taste
- 3 jalapeño peppers, chopped
- ¾ cup butter, chopped

Instructions:
1. Arrange the "Crisper Basket" in the pot of Ninja Foodi Grill.
2. Close the Ninja Foodi Grill with lid and select "Roast".
3. Set the temperature to 380 degrees F to preheat.
4. Press "Start/Stop" to begin preheating.
5. Coat the halibut fillets with ginger-garlic paste and then season with salt and black pepper.
6. When the display shows "Add Food" open the lid and place the halibut fillets into the "Crisper Basket" in a single layer and top with jalapeño peppers, followed by the butter.
7. Close the Ninja Foodi Grill with lid and set the time for 30 minutes.
8. Press "Start/Stop" to begin cooking.
9. When the cooking time is completed, press "Start/Stop" to stop cooking and open the lid.
10. Serve hot.

Nutritional Information per Serving:
Calories: 443 | Fat: 37.4g | Saturated Fat: 22.2g | Carbohydrates: 2.5g | Sugar: 0.5g | Protein: 24.6g

82. Sweet & Sour Salmon

⏰ Prep Time 15 m | ⏰ Cooking Time 12 m | 4 Servings

Ingredients:
- 1/3 cup soy sauce
- 1/3 cup honey
- 3 teaspoons rice wine vinegar
- 1 teaspoon water
- 4 (3½-ounces) salmon fillets

Instructions:
1. In a small bowl, mix together the soy sauce, honey, vinegar, and water.
2. In another bowl, reserve about half of the mixture.
3. Add salmon fillets in the remaining mixture and coat well.
4. Cover the bowl and refrigerate to marinate for about 2 hours.
5. Arrange the "Crisper Basket" in the pot of Ninja Foodi Grill.
6. Close the Ninja Foodi Grill with lid and select "Air Crisp".
7. Set the temperature to 350 degrees F to preheat.
8. Press "Start/Stop" to begin preheating.
9. When the display shows "Add Food" open the lid and place the salmon fillets into the "Crisper Basket".
10. Close the Ninja Foodi Grill with lid and set the time for 12 minutes.
11. Press "Start/Stop" to begin cooking.
12. Flip the salmon fillets once halfway through and coat with the reserved marinade after every 3 minutes.
13. When the cooking time is completed, press "Start/Stop" to stop cooking and open the lid.
14. Serve hot.

Nutritional Information per Serving:
Calories: 462 | Fat: 12.3g | Saturated Fat: 1.8g | Carbohydrates: 49.8g | Sugar: 47.1g | Protein: 41.3g

83. Glazed Haddock

⏰ Prep Time 15 m | ⏰ Cooking Time 15 m | 4 Servings

Ingredients:

- 1 garlic clove, minced
- ¼ teaspoon fresh ginger, grated finely
- ½ cup low-sodium soy sauce
- ¼ cup fresh orange juice
- 2 tablespoons fresh lime juice
- ½ cup cooking wine
- ¼ cup sugar
- ¼ teaspoon red pepper flakes, crushed
- 1 pound haddock steaks

Instructions:

1. In a pan, add all the ingredients except for haddock steaks and bring to a boil.
2. Cook for about 3-4 minutes, stirring continuously.
3. Remove from the heat and set aside to cool.
4. In a resealable bag, add half of marinade and haddock steaks.
5. Seal the bag and shake to coat well.
6. Refrigerate for about 30 minutes.
7. Remove the fish steaks from bag, reserving the remaining marinade.
8. Arrange the greased "Crisper Basket" in the pot of Ninja Foodi Grill.
9. Close the Ninja Foodi Grill with lid and select "Air Crisp".
10. Set the temperature to 390 degrees F to preheat.
11. Press "Start/Stop" to begin preheating.
12. When the display shows "Add Food" open the lid and place the haddock steaks into the "Crisper Basket".
13. Close the Ninja Foodi Grill with lid and set the time for 11 minutes.
14. Press "Start/Stop" to begin cooking.
15. After 4 minutes of cooking, flip the salmon steaks.
16. When the cooking time is completed, press "Start/Stop" to stop cooking and open the lid.
17. Place the haddock steak onto a serving platter.
18. Immediately, coat the haddock steak with the remaining glaze and serve.

Nutritional Information per Serving:
Calories: 218 | Fat: 1.1g | Saturated Fat: 0.2g | Carbohydrates: 17.4g | Sugar: 16.1g | Protein: 29.7g

84. Simple Cod

⏰ Prep Time 10 m | ⏰ Cooking Time 10 m | 2 Servings

Ingredients:

- 2 (6-ounce) cod fillets
- Salt and freshly ground black pepper, to taste

Instructions:

1. Season the cod fillets with salt and black pepper.
2. Arrange the "Grill Grate" in the pot of Ninja Foodi Grill.
3. Close the Ninja Foodi Grill with lid and select "Grill" on "Medium" to preheat.
4. Press "Start/Stop" to begin preheating.
5. When the display shows "Add Food" open the lid and grease the "Grill Grate".
6. Place the cod fillets onto the "Grill Grate".
7. With your hands, gently press down each cod fillet.
8. Close the Ninja Foodi Grill with lid and set the time for 12 minutes.
9. Press "Start/Stop" to begin cooking.
10. When the cooking time is completed, press "Start/Stop" to stop cooking and open the lid.
11. Serve hot.

Nutritional Information per Serving:

Calories: 137 | Fat: 1.5g | Saturated Fat: g | Carbohydrates: 0g | Sugar: 0g | Protein: 30.4g

85. Crusted Sole

⏰ Prep Time 15 m | ⏰ Cooking Time 15 m | 2 Servings

Ingredients:

- 2 teaspoons mayonnaise
- 1 teaspoon fresh chives, minced
- 3 tablespoons Parmesan cheese, shredded
- 2 tablespoons panko breadcrumbs
- Salt and freshly ground black pepper, to taste
- 2 (4-ounce) sole fillets

Instructions:

1. In a shallow plate, mix together the mayonnaise and chives.
2. In another shallow plate, mix together the cheese, breadcrumbs, salt and black pepper.
3. Coat the fish fillets with mayonnaise mixture and then roll in cheese mixture.
4. Arrange the fish fillets onto the greased "Baking pan" in a single layer.
5. Arrange the "Crisper Basket" in the pot of Ninja Foodi Grill.
6. Close the Ninja Foodi Grill with lid and select "Roast".
7. Set the temperature to 450 degrees F to preheat.
8. Press "Start/Stop" to begin preheating.
9. When the display shows "Add Food" open the lid and place the fish fillets into the "Crisper Basket".
10. Close the Ninja Foodi Grill with lid and set the time for 15 minutes.
11. Press "Start/Stop" to begin cooking.
12. When the cooking time is completed, press "Start/Stop" to stop cooking and open the lid.
13. Serve hot.

Nutritional Information per Serving:

Calories: 584 | Fat: 14.6g | Saturated Fat: 5.2g | Carbohydrates: 16.7g | Sugar: 0.2g | Protein: 33.2g

86. Cod & Veggie Parcel

◐ Prep Time 15 m | ◐ Cooking Time 15 m | 2 Servings

Ingredients:

- 2 tablespoons butter, melted
- 1 tablespoon fresh lemon juice
- ½ teaspoon dried tarragon
- Salt and freshly ground black pepper, to taste
- ½ cup red bell peppers, seeded and sliced thinly
- ½ cup carrots, peeled and julienned
- ½ cup fennel bulbs, julienned
- 2 (5-ounce) frozen cod fillets, thawed
- 1 tablespoon olive oil

Instructions:

1. In a large bowl, place the butter, lemon juice, tarragon, salt, and black pepper and mix well.
2. Add the bell pepper, carrot, and fennel bulb and coat with the mixture generously.
3. Arrange 2 large parchment squares onto a smooth surface.
4. Coat the cod fillets with oil and then sprinkle evenly with salt and black pepper.
5. Arrange 1 cod fillet onto each parchment square and top each with the vegetables evenly.
6. Top with any remaining sauce from the bowl.
7. Fold the parchment paper and crimp the sides to secure fish and vegetables.
8. Arrange the "Crisper Basket" in the pot of Ninja Foodi Grill.
9. Close the Ninja Foodi Grill with lid and select "Air Crisp"
10. Set the temperature to 350 degrees F to preheat.
11. Press "Start/Stop" to begin preheating.
12. When the display shows "Add Food" open the lid and place the fish parcels into the "Crisper Basket".
13. Close the Ninja Foodi Grill with lid and set the time for 15 minutes.
14. Press "Start/Stop" to begin cooking.
15. When the cooking time is completed, press "Start/Stop" to stop cooking and open the lid.
16. Transfer the parcels onto serving plates.
17. Carefully open each parcel and serve warm.

Nutritional Information per Serving:

Calories: 306 | Fat: 20g | Saturated Fat: 8.4g | Carbohydrates: 6.8g | Sugar: 3g | Protein: 26.3g

87. Spicy Catfish

⏰ Prep Time 10 m | ⏰ Cooking Time 13 m | 2 Servings

Ingredients:

- 2 tablespoons almond flour
- 1 teaspoon red chili powder
- ½ teaspoon paprika
- ½ teaspoon garlic powder
- Salt, to taste
- 2 (6-ounce) catfish fillets
- 1 tablespoon olive oil

Instructions:

1. In a bowl, mix together the flour, paprika, garlic powder and salt.
2. Add the catfish fillets and coat with the mixture evenly.
3. Now, coat each fillet with oil.
4. Arrange the greased "Crisper Basket" in the pot of Ninja Foodi Grill.
5. Close the Ninja Foodi Grill with lid and select "Air Crisp"
6. Set the temperature to 400 degrees F to preheat.
7. Press "Start/Stop" to begin preheating.
8. When the display shows "Add Food" open the lid and place the catfish fillets into the "Crisper Basket".
9. Close the Ninja Foodi Grill with lid and set the time for 13 minutes.
10. Press "Start/Stop" to begin cooking.
11. Flip the fish fillets once halfway through.
12. When the cooking time is completed, press "Start/Stop" to stop cooking and open the lid.
13. Serve hot.

Nutritional Information per Serving:
Calories: 458|Fat: 34.2g|Saturated Fat: 4.4g|Carbohydrates: 7.5g|Sugar: 1.3g|Protein: 32.8g

88. Ranch Tilapia

⏰ Prep Time 10 m | ⏰ Cooking Time 13 m | 4 Servings

Ingredients:

- ¾ cup cornflakes, crushed
- 1 (1-ounce) packet dry ranch-style dressing mix
- 2½ tablespoons vegetable oil
- 2 eggs
- 4 (6-ounce) tilapia fillets

Instructions:

1. In a shallow bowl, beat the eggs.
2. In another bowl, add the cornflakes, ranch dressing, and oil and mix until a crumbly mixture forms.
3. Dip the fish fillets into egg and then coat with the breadcrumbs mixture.
4. Arrange the greased "Crisper Basket" in the pot of Ninja Foodi Grill.
5. Close the Ninja Foodi Grill with lid and select "Air Crisp".
6. Set the temperature to 356 degrees F to preheat.
7. Press "Start/Stop" to begin preheating.
8. When the display shows "Add Food" open the lid and place the tilapia fillets into the "Crisper Basket".
9. Close the Ninja Foodi Grill with lid and set the time for 13 minutes.
10. Press "Start/Stop" to begin cooking.
11. When the cooking time is completed, press "Start/Stop" to stop cooking and open the lid.
12. Serve hot.

Nutritional Information per Serving:

Calories: 267 | Fat: 12.2g | Saturated Fat: 3g | Carbohydrates: 5.1g | Sugar: 0.9g | Protein: 34.9g

89. Lemony Shrimp

⏰ Prep Time 15 m | ⏰ Cooking Time 8 m | 3 Servings

Ingredients:

- 2 tablespoons fresh lemon juice
- 1 tablespoon olive oil
- 1 teaspoon lemon pepper
- ¼ teaspoon paprika
- ¼ teaspoon garlic powder
- 12 ounces medium shrimp, peeled and deveined

Instructions:

1. In a large bowl, add all the ingredients except the shrimp and mix until well combined.
2. Add the shrimp and toss to coat well.
3. Arrange the greased "Crisper Basket" in the pot of Ninja Foodi Grill.
4. Close the Ninja Foodi Grill with lid and select "Air Crisp".
5. Set the temperature to 400 degrees F to preheat.
6. Press "Start/Stop" to begin preheating.
7. When the display shows "Add Food" open the lid and place the shrimp into the "Crisper Basket".
8. Close the Ninja Foodi Grill with lid and set the time for 8 minutes.
9. Press "Start/Stop" to begin cooking.
10. When the cooking time is completed, press "Start/Stop" to stop cooking and open the lid.
11. Serve hot.

Nutritional Information per Serving:

Calories: 154 | Fat: 6.1g | Saturated Fat: 0.8g | Carbohydrates: 0.9g | Sugar: 0.3g | Protein: 24.5g

90. Shrimp Scampi

⏰ Prep Time 15 m | ⏰ Cooking Time 5 m | 3 Servings

Ingredients:

- 4 tablespoons salted butter
- 1 tablespoon fresh lemon juice
- 1 tablespoon garlic, minced
- 2 teaspoons red pepper flakes, crushed
- 1 pound shrimp, peeled and deveined
- 2 tablespoons fresh basil, chopped
- 1 tablespoon fresh chives, chopped
- 2 tablespoons chicken broth

Instructions:

1. Arrange a 7-inch round baking pan in the "Crisper Basket".
2. Now, arrange the "Crisper Basket" in the pot of Ninja Foodi Grill.
3. Close the Ninja Foodi Grill with lid and select "Air Crisp".
4. Set the temperature to 325 degrees F to preheat.
5. Press "Start/Stop" to begin preheating.
6. When the display shows "Add Food" open the lid and carefully remove the pan from Ninja Foodi.
7. In the heated pan, place the butter, lemon juice, garlic, and red pepper flakes and mix well.
8. Place the pan into the "Crisper Basket".
9. Close the Ninja Foodi Grill with lid and set the time for 7 minutes.
10. Press "Start/Stop" to begin cooking.
11. After 2 minutes of cooking, stir in the shrimp, basil, chives and broth.
12. When cooking time is completed, press "Start/Stop" to stop cooking and open the lid.
13. Place the pan onto a wire rack for about 1 minute.
14. Stir the mixture and serve hot.

Nutritional Information per Serving:

Calories: 327 | Fat: 18.3g | Saturated Fat: 10.6g | Carbohydrates: 4.2g | Sugar: 0.3g | Protein: 35.3g

91. Shrimp Kabobs

⏰ Prep Time 15 m | ⏰ Cooking Time 8 m | 2 Servings

Ingredients:

- ¾ pound shrimp, peeled and deveined
- 2 tablespoons fresh lemon juice
- 1 teaspoon garlic, minced
- ½ teaspoon paprika
- ½ teaspoon ground cumin
- Salt and freshly ground black pepper, to taste
- 1 tablespoon fresh cilantro, chopped

Instructions:

1. In a bowl, mix together the lemon juice, garlic, and spices.
2. Add the shrimp and mix well.
3. Thread the shrimp onto presoaked wooden skewers.
4. Arrange the greased "Crisper Basket" in the pot of Ninja Foodi Grill.
5. Close the Ninja Foodi Grill with lid and select "Air Crisp".
6. Set the temperature to 350 degrees F to preheat.
7. Press "Start/Stop" to begin preheating.
8. When the display shows "Add Food" open the lid and place the shrimp skewers into the "Crisper Basket".
9. Close the Ninja Foodi Grill with lid and set the time for 8 minutes.
10. Press "Start/Stop" to begin cooking.
11. Flip the shrimp kabobs once halfway through.
12. When cooking time is completed, press "Start/Stop" to stop cooking and open the lid.
13. Transfer the shrimp kabobs onto serving plates.
14. Garnish with fresh cilantro and serve immediately.

Nutritional Information per Serving:
Calories: 212 | Fat: 3.2g | Saturated Fat: 1g | Carbohydrates: 3.9g | Sugar: 0.4g | Protein: 39.1g

92. Thyme Scallops

⏰ Prep Time 15 m | ⏱ Cooking Time 4 m | 2 Servings

Ingredients:

- ¾ pound sea scallops, cleaned and patted very dry
- 1 tablespoon butter, melted
- ½ tablespoon fresh thyme, minced
- Salt and freshly ground black pepper, to taste

Instructions:

1. In a large bowl, place the scallops, butter, thyme, salt, and black pepper and toss to coat well.
2. Arrange the "Crisper Basket" in the pot of Ninja Foodi Grill.
3. Close the Ninja Foodi Grill with lid and select "Air Crisp".
4. Set the temperature to 390 degrees F to preheat.
5. Press "Start/Stop" to begin preheating.
6. When the display shows "Add Food" open the lid and place the scallops into the "Crisper Basket".
7. Close the Ninja Foodi Grill with lid and set the time for 4 minutes.
8. Press "Start/Stop" to begin cooking.
9. When the cooking time is completed, press "Start/Stop" to stop cooking and open the lid.
10. Serve hot.

Nutritional Information per Serving:
Calories: 135|Fat: 4.7g|Saturated Fat: 2.5g|Carbohydrates: 3g|Sugar: 0g|Protein: 19.1g

93. Scallops in Capers Sauce

⏰ Prep Time 15 m | ⏱ Cooking Time 6 m | 3 Servings

Ingredients:

- 12 (1-ounce) sea scallops, cleaned and patted very dry
- Salt and freshly ground black pepper, to taste
- ¼ cup olive oil
- 2 tablespoons fresh parsley, finely chopped
- 2 teaspoons capers, finely chopped
- 1 teaspoon fresh lemon zest, finely grated
- ½ teaspoon garlic, finely chopped

Instructions:

1. Arrange the greased "Crisper Basket" in the pot of Ninja Foodi Grill.
2. Close the Ninja Foodi Grill with lid and select "Air Crisp".
3. Set the temperature to 400 degrees F to preheat.
4. Press "Start/Stop" to begin preheating.
5. Season each scallop with salt and black pepper evenly.
6. When the display shows "Add Food" open the lid and place the scallops into the "Crisper Basket".
7. Close the Ninja Foodi Grill with lid and set the time for 6 minutes.
8. Press "Start/Stop" to begin cooking.
9. Meanwhile, for sauce: in a bowl, mix the remaining ingredients.
10. When cooking time is completed, press "Start/Stop" to stop cooking and open the lid
11. Transfer the scallops onto serving plates.
12. Top with the sauce and serve immediately.

Nutritional Information per Serving:
Calories: 246|Fat: 17.7g|Saturated Fat: 2.5g|Carbohydrates: 3.2g|Sugar: 0.1gProtein: 21.2g

94. Scallops with Spinach

⏰ Prep Time 15 m | ⏰ Cooking Time 10 m | 3 Servings

Ingredients:

- 1 (10-ounce) package frozen spinach, thawed and drained
- 12 sea scallops
- Olive oil cooking spray
- Salt and freshly ground black pepper, to taste
- ¾ cup heavy whipping cream
- 1 tablespoon tomato paste
- 1 teaspoon garlic, minced
- 1 tablespoon fresh basil, chopped

Instructions:

1. In the bottom of a 7-inch heatproof pan, place the spinach.
2. Spray each scallop with cooking spray and then sprinkle with a little salt and black pepper.
3. Arrange scallops on top of the spinach in a single layer.
4. In a bowl, add the cream, tomato paste, garlic, basil, salt and black pepper and mix well.
5. Place the cream mixture over the spinach and scallops evenly.
6. Arrange the greased "Crisper Basket" in the pot of Ninja Foodi Grill.
7. Close the Ninja Foodi Grill with lid and select "Air Crisp".
8. Set the temperature to 350 degrees F to preheat.
9. Press "Start/Stop" to begin preheating.
10. When the display shows "Add Food" open the lid and place the pan into "Crisper Basket".
11. Close the Ninja Foodi Grill with lid and set the time for 10 minutes.
12. Press "Start/Stop" to begin cooking.
13. When the cooking time is completed, press "Start/Stop" to stop cooking and open the lid.
14. Serve hot.

Nutritional Information per Serving:
Calories: 237 | Fat: 12.4g | Saturated Fat: 7.1g | Carbohydrates: 8.4g | Sugar: 1.1g | Protein: 23.8g

95. Seafood Pasta

⏰ Prep Time 20 m | ⏰ Cooking Time 18 m | 4 Servings

Ingredients:
- 14 ounces pasta (of your choice)
- 4 tablespoons pesto, divided
- 4 (4-ounce) salmon steaks
- 2 tablespoons olive oil
- ½ pound cherry tomatoes, chopped
- 8 large prawns, peeled and deveined
- 2 tablespoons fresh lemon juice
- 2 tablespoons fresh thyme, chopped

Instructions:
1. In a large pan of salted boiling water, add the pasta and cook for about 8-10 minutes or until desired doneness.
2. Meanwhile, in the bottom of a baking pan, spread 1 tablespoon of pesto.
3. Place salmon steaks and tomatoes over pesto in a single layer and drizzle with the oil.
4. Arrange the prawns on top in a single layer.
5. Drizzle with lemon juice and sprinkle with thyme.
6. Arrange the "Crisper Basket" in the pot of Ninja Foodi Grill.
7. Close the Ninja Foodi Grill with lid and select "Air Crisp".
8. Set the temperature to 390 degrees F to preheat.
9. Press "Start/Stop" to begin preheating.
10. When the display shows "Add Food" open the lid and place the pan into the "Crisper Basket".
11. Close the Ninja Foodi Grill with lid and set the time for 8 minutes.
12. Press "Start/Stop" to begin cooking.
13. When the cooking time is completed, press "Start/Stop" to stop cooking and open the lid.
14. Drain the pasta and transfer into a large bowl.
15. Add the remaining pesto and toss to coat well.
16. Divide the pasta onto serving plates and top with salmon mixture.
17. Serve immediately.

Nutritional Information per Serving:
Calories: 592 | Fat: 23.2g | Saturated Fat: 3.8g | Carbohydrates: 58.7g | Sugar: 2.7g | Protein: 37.9g

VEGETARIAN AND VEGAN RECIPES

96. Veggie Ratatouille

⏰ Prep Time 15 m | ⏰ Cooking Time 15 m | 4 Servings

Ingredients:
- 1 green bell pepper, seeded and chopped
- 1 yellow bell pepper, seeded and chopped
- 1 eggplant, chopped
- 1 zucchini, chopped
- 3 tomatoes, chopped
- 2 small onions, chopped
- 2 garlic cloves, minced
- 2 tablespoons Herbs de Provence
- 1 tablespoon olive oil
- 1 tablespoon balsamic vinegar
- Salt and freshly ground black pepper, to taste

Instructions:
1. In a large bowl, add the vegetables, garlic, Herbs de Provence, oil, vinegar, salt, and black pepper and toss to coat well.
2. Transfer vegetable mixture into a greased baking pan.
3. Arrange the "Crisper Basket" in the pot of Ninja Foodi Grill.
4. Close the Ninja Foodi Grill with lid and select "Air Crisp".
5. Set the temperature to 355 degrees F to preheat.
6. Press "Start/Stop" to begin preheating.
7. When the display shows "Add Food" open the lid and place the pan into the "Crisper Basket".
8. Close the Ninja Foodi Grill with lid and set the time for 15 minutes.
9. Press "Start/Stop" to begin cooking.
10. When the cooking time is completed, press "Start/Stop" to stop cooking and open the lid.
11. Serve hot.

Nutritional Information per Serving:
Calories: 119 | Fat: 4.2g | Saturated Fat: 0.6g | Carbohydrates: 20.3g | Sugar: 11.2g | Protein: 3.6g

97. Nutty Acorn Squash

⏰ Prep Time 10 m | ⏰ Cooking Time 25 m | 2 Servings

Ingredients:
- 1 medium acorn squash
- 2 teaspoons olive oil
- 2 tablespoons pecans, chopped
- 1 tablespoon brown sugar
- ½ teaspoon ground cinnamon
- 1/8 teaspoon ground cloves

Instructions:
1. Cut the acorn squash in half lengthwise.
2. Brush the flesh side of each squash half with oil.
3. In a bowl, add the remaining ingredients and mix.
4. Arrange the "Crisper Basket" in the pot of Ninja Foodi Grill.
5. Close the Ninja Foodi Grill with lid and select "Air Crisp".
6. Set the temperature to 375 degrees F to preheat.
7. Press "Start/Stop" to begin preheating.
8. When the display shows "Add Food" open the lid and place the squash halves, cut side up into the "Crisper Basket".
9. Close the Ninja Foodi Grill with lid and set the time for 25 minutes.
10. Press "Start/Stop" to begin cooking.
11. When the cooking time is completed, press "Start/Stop" to stop cooking and open the lid.
12. Serve warm.

Nutritional Information per Serving:
Calories: 254 | Fat: 11.1g | Saturated Fat: 1.4g | Carbohydrates: 41.6g | Sugar: 4.7g | Protein: 3.7g

98. Vegetarian Stuffed Bell Peppers

⏰ Prep Time 15 m | ⏰ Cooking Time 15 m | 5 Servings

Ingredients:

- ½ of small bell pepper, seeded and chopped
- 1 (15-ounce) can diced tomatoes with juice
- 1 (15-ounce) can red kidney beans, rinsed and drained
- 1 cup cooked rice
- 1½ teaspoons Italian seasoning
- 5 large bell peppers, tops removed and seeded
- ½ cup mozzarella cheese, shredded
- 1 tablespoon Parmesan cheese, grated

Instructions:

1. In a bowl, mix together the chopped bell pepper, tomatoes with juice, beans, rice, and Italian seasoning.
2. Stuff each bell pepper with the rice mixture.
3. Arrange the greased "Crisper Basket" in the pot of Ninja Foodi Grill.
4. Close the Ninja Foodi Grill with lid and select "Air Crisp".
5. Set the temperature to 360 degrees F to preheat.
6. Press "Start/Stop" to begin preheating.
7. When the display shows "Add Food" open the lid and place the bell peppers into the "Crisper Basket".
8. Close the Ninja Foodi Grill with lid and set the time for 15 minutes.
9. Press "Start/Stop" to begin cooking.
10. Meanwhile, in a bowl, mix together the mozzarella and Parmesan cheese.
11. After 12 minutes of cooking, top each bell pepper with cheese mixture.
12. When cooking time is completed, press "Start/Stop" to stop cooking and open the lid.
13. Transfer the bell peppers onto a serving platter and serve warm.

Nutritional Information per Serving:

Calories: 404 | Fat: 3.4g | Saturated Fat: 13.4g | Carbohydrates: 2.1g | Sugar: 10.2g | Protein: 23.9g

99. Stuffed Pumpkin

⏰ Prep Time 20 m | ⏰ Cooking Time 30 m | 5 Servings

Ingredients:

- 1 sweet potato, peeled and chopped
- 1 parsnip, peeled and chopped
- 1 carrot, peeled and chopped
- ½ cup fresh peas, shelled
- 1 onion, chopped
- 2 garlic cloves, minced
- 1 egg, beaten
- 2 teaspoons mixed dried herbs
- Salt and freshly ground black pepper, to taste
- ½ of butternut pumpkin, seeded

Instructions:

1. In a large bowl, mix together the vegetables, garlic, egg, herbs, salt, and black pepper.
2. Stuff the pumpkin half with vegetable mixture.
3. Arrange the "Crisper Basket" in the pot of Ninja Foodi Grill.
4. Close the Ninja Foodi Grill with lid and select "Air Crisp".
5. Set the temperature to 355 degrees F to preheat.
6. Press "Start/Stop" to begin preheating.
7. When the display shows "Add Food" open the lid and place the pumpkin into the "Crisper Basket".
8. Close the Ninja Foodi Grill with lid and set the time for 30 minutes.
9. Press "Start/Stop" to begin cooking.
10. When the cooking time is completed, press "Start/Stop" to stop cooking and open the lid.
11. Transfer the pumpkin onto a serving platter and set aside to cool slightly before serving.

Nutritional Information per Serving:

Calories: 223 | Fat: 1.3g | Saturated Fat: 0.3g | Carbohydrates: 53g | Sugar: 12g | Protein: 6g

100. Vegetarian Loaf

⏰ Prep Time 20 m | ⏰ Cooking Time 1 h 30 m | 6 Servings

Ingredients:

- 1 (14½-ounce) can vegetable broth
- ¾ cup brown lentils, rinsed
- 1 tablespoon olive oil
- 1¾ cups carrots, peeled and shredded
- 1 cup fresh mushrooms, chopped
- 1 cup onion, chopped
- 1 tablespoon fresh parsley, minced
- 1 tablespoon fresh basil, minced
- ½ cup cooked brown rice
- 1 cup mozzarella cheese, shredded
- 1 large egg
- 1 large egg white
- Salt and freshly ground black pepper, to taste
- 2 tablespoons tomato paste
- 2 tablespoons water

Instructions:

1. In a pan, place the broth over medium-high heat and bring to a boil.
2. Stir in the lentils and again bring to a boil.
3. Reduce the heat to low and simmer, covered for about 30 minutes.
4. Remove from the heat and set aside to cool slightly.
5. Meanwhile, in a large skillet, heat the oil over medium heat and sauté the carrots, mushrooms and onion for about 10 minutes.
6. Stir in herbs and remove from the heat.
7. Transfer the veggie mixture into a large bowl and set aside to cool slightly.
8. After cooling, add the lentils, rice, cheese, egg, egg white and seasonings and lentils and mix until well combined.
9. In a small bowl, stir together the tomato paste and water.
10. Place the mixture into a greased parchment paper-lined loaf pan and top with water mixture.
11. Arrange the "Crisper Basket" in the pot of Ninja Foodi Grill.
12. Close the Ninja Foodi Grill with lid and select "Bake".
13. Set the temperature to 350 degrees F to preheat.
14. Press "Start/Stop" to begin preheating.
15. When the display shows "Add Food" open the lid and place the pan into the "Crisper Basket".
16. Close the Ninja Foodi Grill with lid and set the time for 50 minutes.
17. Press "Start/Stop" to begin cooking.
18. When the cooking time is completed, press "Start/Stop" to stop cooking and open the lid.
19. Place the loaf pan onto a wire rack for about 10 minutes before slicing.
20. Carefully invert the loaf onto the wire rack.
21. Cut into desired sized slices and serve.

Nutritional Information per Serving:

Calories: 229 | Fat: 5.1g | Saturated Fat: 1.3g | Carbohydrates: 33.4g | Sugar: 4g | Protein: 12.8g

101. Beans & Veggie Burgers

⏰ Prep Time 20 m | ⏰ Cooking Time 21 m | 4 Servings

Ingredients:

- 1 cup cooked black beans
- 2 cups boiled potatoes, peeled and mashed
- 1 cup fresh spinach, chopped
- 1 cup fresh mushrooms, chopped
- 2 teaspoons Chile lime seasoning
- Olive oil cooking spray

Instructions:

1. In a large bowl, add the beans, potatoes, spinach, mushrooms, and seasoning and with your hands, mix until well combined.
2. Make 4 equal-sized patties from the mixture.
3. Arrange the greased "Crisper Basket" in the pot of Ninja Foodi Grill.
4. Close the Ninja Foodi Grill with lid and select "Air Crisp".
5. Set the temperature to 370 degrees to preheat.
6. Press "Start/Stop" to begin preheating.
7. When the display shows "Add Food" open the lid and place the patties into the "Crisper Basket".
8. Close the Ninja Foodi Grill with lid and set the time for 18 minutes.
9. Press "Start/Stop" to begin cooking.
10. After 12 minutes of cooking, flip the patties once.
11. After 18 minutes of cooking, set the temperature to 390 degrees F for 3 minutes.
12. When the cooking time is completed, press "Start/Stop" to stop cooking and open the lid.
13. Serve hot.

Nutritional Information per Serving:
Calories: 114 | Fat: 0.4g | Saturated Fat: 0.1g | Carbohydrates: 22.8g | Sugar: 1.2g | Protein: 5.8g

102. Tofu with Orange Sauce

⏰ Prep Time 15 m | ⏰ Cooking Time 20 m | 4 Servings

Ingredients:

For Tofu:
- 1 pound extra-firm tofu, pressed, drained and cubed
- 1 tablespoon cornstarch
- 1 tablespoon tamari

For Sauce:
- ½ cup water
- 1/3 cup fresh orange juice
- 1 tablespoon honey
- 1 teaspoon orange zest, grated
- 1 teaspoon garlic, minced
- 1 teaspoon fresh ginger, minced
- 2 teaspoons cornstarch
- ¼ teaspoon red pepper flakes, crushed

Instructions:

1. In a bowl, add the tofu, cornstarch, and tamari and toss to coat well.
2. Set the tofu aside to marinate for at least 15 minutes.
3. Arrange the greased "Crisper Basket" in the pot of Ninja Foodi Grill.
4. Close the Ninja Foodi Grill with lid and select "Air Crisp".
5. Set the temperature to 390 degrees F to preheat.
6. Press "Start/Stop" to begin preheating.
7. When the display shows "Add Food" open the lid and place the tofu cubes into the "Crisper Basket".
8. Close the Ninja Foodi Grill with lid and set the time for 10 minutes.
9. Press "Start/Stop" to begin cooking.
10. Meanwhile, for the sauce: in a small pan, add all the ingredients over medium-high heat and bring to a boil, stirring continuously.
11. When the cooking time is completed, press "Start/Stop" to stop cooking and open the lid.
12. Transfer the tofu into a serving bowl.
13. Add the sauce and gently stir to combine.
14. Serve immediately.

Nutritional Information per Serving:
Calories: 150 | Fat: 6.7g | Saturated Fat: 0.6g | Carbohydrates: 13.3g | Sugar: 6.7g | Protein: 12g

103. Mac n' Cheese

⏰ Prep Time 10 m | ⏰ Cooking Time 25 m | 4 Servings

Ingredients:

- 2 cups cheddar cheese, shredded and divided
- 1 teaspoon cornstarch
- 2 cup heavy whipping cream
- 2 cups dry macaroni

Instructions:

1. In a bowl, place 1½ cups of cheese and cornstarch and mix well. Set aside.
2. In another bowl, place the remaining cheese, whipping cream and macaroni and mix well.
3. Transfer the macaroni mixture into a baking pan.
4. With a piece of foil, cover the pan.
5. Arrange the "Crisper Basket" in the pot of Ninja Foodi Grill.
6. Close the Ninja Foodi Grill with lid and select "Air Crisp".
7. Set the temperature to 310 degrees F to preheat.
8. Press "Start/Stop" to begin preheating.
9. When the display shows "Add Food" open the lid and place the baking pan into the "Crisper Basket".
10. Close the Ninja Foodi Grill with lid and set the time for 25 minutes.
11. After 15 minutes of cooking, remove the foil and top the macaroni mixture with cornstarch mixture.
12. When the cooking time is completed, press "Start/Stop" to stop cooking and open the lid.
13. Serve warm.

Nutritional Information per Serving:

Calories: 593 | Fat: 41.6g | Saturated Fat: 25.9g | Carbohydrates: 34.4g | Sugar: 1.5g | Protein: 20.8g

SIDE DISHES RECIPES

104. Stuffed Tomatoes

⏱ Prep Time 15 m | ⏱ Cooking Time 14 m | 2 Servings

Ingredients:

- 2 large tomatoes
- ½ cup broccoli, chopped finely
- ½ cup cheddar cheese, shredded
- 1 tablespoon unsalted butter, melted
- ½ teaspoon dried thyme, crushed

Instructions:

1. Carefully cut the top of each tomato and scoop out pulp and seeds.
2. In a bowl, place the chopped broccoli and cheese and mix.
3. Stuff each tomato with broccoli mixture evenly.
4. Arrange the "Crisper Basket" in the pot of Ninja Foodi Grill.
5. Close the Ninja Foodi Grill with lid and select "Air Crisp".
6. Set the temperature to 355 degrees F to preheat.
7. Press "Start/Stop" to begin preheating.
8. When the display shows "Add Food" open the lid and place the tomatoes into the "Crisper Basket".
9. Drizzle the tomatoes with the butter.
10. Close the Ninja Foodi Grill with lid and set the time for 15 minutes.
11. Press "Start/Stop" to begin cooking.
12. When the cooking time is completed, press "Start/Stop" to stop cooking and open the lid.
13. Serve with the garnishing of thyme.

Nutritional Information per Serving:

Calories: 206 | Fat: 15.6g | Saturated Fat: 9.7g | Carbohydrates: 9.1g | Sugar: 5.3g | Protein: 9.4g

105. Pesto Tomatoes

⏰ Prep Time 15 m | ⏱ Cooking Time 14 m | 4 Servings

Ingredients:

For Pesto:
- ½ cup olive oil
- 3 tablespoons pine nuts
- Salt, to taste
- ½ cup fresh basil, chopped
- ½ cup fresh parsley, chopped
- 1 garlic clove, chopped
- ½ cup Parmesan cheese, grated

For Tomatoes:
- 4 heirloom tomatoes, cut into ½ inch thick slices
- 8 ounces feta cheese, cut into ½ inch thick slices
- ½ cup red onions, thinly sliced
- 1 tablespoon olive oil
- Salt, to taste

Instructions:

1. In a food processor, add the pine nuts, fresh herbs, garlic, Parmesan, and salt and pulse until just combined.
2. While motor is running, slowly add the oil and pulse until smooth.
3. Transfer the pesto into a bowl, and refrigerate, covered until serving.
4. Spread about one tablespoons of pesto onto each tomato slice.
5. Top each tomato slice with one feta and onion slice and drizzle with oil.
6. Arrange the "Crisper Basket" in the pot of Ninja Foodi Grill.
7. Close the Ninja Foodi Grill with lid and select "Air Crisp".
8. Set the temperature to 390 degrees F to preheat.
9. Press "Start/Stop" to begin preheating.
10. When the display shows "Add Food" open the lid and place the scallops into the "Crisper Basket".
11. Close the Ninja Foodi Grill with lid and set the time for 14 minutes.
12. Press "Start/Stop" to begin cooking.
13. When the cooking time is completed, press "Start/Stop" to stop cooking and open the lid.
14. Transfer the tomato slices onto serving plates.
15. Sprinkle with a little salt and serve with the remaining pesto.

Nutritional Information per Serving:

Calories: 616 | Fat: 56.3g | Saturated Fat: 18.3g | Carbohydrates: 12.1g | Sugar: 6.5g | Protein: 22.5g

106. Cheesy Spinach

⏱ Prep Time 10 m | ⏱ Cooking Time 15 m | 4 Servings

Ingredients:

- 1 pound fresh spinach, chopped
- 4 tablespoons butter, melted
- Salt and freshly ground black pepper, to taste
- 1 cup feta cheese, crumbled
- 1 teaspoon fresh lemon zest, grated

Instructions:

1. In a bowl, add the spinach, butter, salt and black pepper and mix well.
2. Arrange the "Crisper Basket" in the pot of Ninja Foodi Grill.
3. Close the Ninja Foodi Grill with lid and select "Air Crisp".
4. Set the temperature to 340 degrees F to preheat.
5. Press "Start/Stop" to begin preheating.
6. When the display shows "Add Food" open the lid and place the spinach mixture into the "Crisper Basket".
7. Close the Ninja Foodi Grill with lid and set the time for 15 minutes.
8. Press "Start/Stop" to begin cooking.
9. When the cooking time is completed, press "Start/Stop" to stop cooking and open the lid.
10. Immediately transfer the spinach mixture into a bowl.
11. Add the cheese and lemon zest and stir to combine.
12. Serve hot.

Nutritional Information per Serving:
Calories: 227 | Fat: 19.9g | Saturated Fat: 13g | Carbohydrates: 5.8g | Sugar: 2.1g | Protein: 8.7g

107. Herbed Mushrooms

⏰ Prep Time 10 m | ⏱ Cooking Time 8 m | 2 Servings

Ingredients:
- 8 ounces button mushrooms, stemmed
- 2 tablespoons olive oil
- 2 tablespoons Italian dried mixed herbs
- Salt and freshly ground black pepper, to taste
- 1 teaspoon dried dill

Instructions:
1. Wash and trim thin slices from the ends of the stems.
2. In a bowl, mix together the mushrooms, dried herbs, oil, salt and black pepper.
3. Arrange the greased "Crisper Basket" in the pot of Ninja Foodi Grill.
4. Close the Ninja Foodi Grill with lid and select "Air Crisp".
5. Set the temperature to 355 degrees F to preheat.
6. Press "Start/Stop" to begin preheating.
7. When the display shows "Add Food" open the lid and place the mushrooms hollow part upwards into the "Crisper Basket".
8. Close the Ninja Foodi Grill with lid and set the time for 8 minutes.
9. Press "Start/Stop" to begin cooking.
10. When cooking time is completed, press "Start/Stop" to stop cooking and open the lid.
11. Serve with the garnishing of dill.

Nutritional Information per Serving:
Calories: 149 | Fat: 14.4g | Saturated Fat: 2g | Carbohydrates: 4.7g | Sugar: 2g | Protein: 3.8g

108. Cheesy Mushrooms

⏰ Prep Time 15 m | ⏰ Cooking Time 8 m | 2 Servings

Ingredients:

- 8 ounces button mushrooms, stemmed
- 2 tablespoons olive oil
- 2 tablespoons Italian dried mixed herbs
- Salt and freshly ground black pepper, to taste
- 2 tablespoons mozzarella cheese, grated
- 2 tablespoons cheddar cheese, grated

Instructions:

1. Wash and trim thin slices from the ends of the stems.
2. In a bowl, mix together the mushrooms, dried herbs, oil, salt and black pepper.
3. Arrange the greased "Crisper Basket" in the pot of Ninja Foodi Grill.
4. Close the Ninja Foodi Grill with lid and select "Air Crisp".
5. Set the temperature to 355 degrees F to preheat.
6. Press "Start/Stop" to begin preheating.
7. When the display shows "Add Food" open the lid and place the mushrooms hollow part upwards into the "Crisper Basket".
8. Close the Ninja Foodi Grill with lid and set the time for 8 minutes.
9. Press "Start/Stop" to begin cooking.
10. When the cooking time is completed, press "Start/Stop" to stop cooking and open the lid.
11. Serve hot.

Nutritional Information per Serving:
Calories: 257 | Fat: 21.7g | Saturated Fat: 6.5g | Carbohydrates: 5.8g | Sugar: 2g | Protein: 13.6g

109. Glazed Carrots

⏰ Prep Time 10 m | ⏰ Cooking Time 12 m | 4 Servings

Ingredients:

- 3 cups carrots, peeled and cut into large chunks
- 1 tablespoon olive oil
- 1 tablespoon honey
- 1 tablespoon fresh thyme, finely chopped
- Salt and freshly ground black pepper, to taste

Instructions:

1. In a bowl, add the carrot, oil, honey, thyme, salt and black pepper and mix until well combined.
2. Arrange the "Crisper Basket" in the pot of Ninja Foodi Grill.
3. Close the Ninja Foodi Grill with lid and select "Air Crisp".
4. Set the temperature to 390 degrees F to preheat.
5. Press "Start/Stop" to begin preheating.
6. When the display shows "Add Food" open the lid and place the carrot chunks into the "Crisper Basket" in a single layer.
7. Close the Ninja Foodi Grill with lid and set the time for 12 minutes.
8. Press "Start/Stop" to begin cooking.
9. When the cooking time is completed, press "Start/Stop" to stop cooking and open the lid.
10. Serve hot.

Nutritional Information per Serving:
Calories: 82 | Fat: 3.6g | Saturated Fat: 0.5g | Carbohydrates: 12.9g | Sugar: 8.4g | Protein: 0.8g

110. Lemony Green Beans

⏱ Prep Time 10 m | ⏱ Cooking Time 12 m | 4 Servings

Ingredients:

- 1 pound fresh green beans, trimmed
- 1 tablespoon butter, melted
- 1 tablespoon fresh lemon juice
- ¼ teaspoon garlic powder
- Salt and freshly ground black pepper, to taste
- ½ teaspoon lemon zest, grated

Instructions:

1. In a large bowl, add all the ingredients except the lemon zest and toss to coat well.
2. Arrange the "Crisper Basket" in the pot of Ninja Foodi Grill.
3. Close the Ninja Foodi Grill with lid and select "Air Crisp".
4. Set the temperature to 400 degrees F to preheat.
5. Press "Start/Stop" to begin preheating.
6. When the display shows "Add Food" open the lid and place the green beans into the "Crisper Basket".
7. Close the Ninja Foodi Grill with lid and set the time for 12 minutes.
8. Press "Start/Stop" to begin cooking.
9. When the cooking time is completed, press "Start/Stop" to stop cooking and open the lid.
10. Serve warm with the garnishing of lemon zest.

Nutritional Information per Serving:

Calories: 62 | Fat: 3.1g | Saturated Fat: 1.9g | Carbohydrates: 8.4g | Sugar: 1.7g | Protein: 2.2g

111. Vinegar Brussels Sprout

⏱ Prep Time 10 m | ⏱ Cooking Time 15 m | 4 Servings

Ingredients:

- 1 pound Brussels sprouts, ends trimmed and cut into bite-sized pieces
- 1 tablespoon balsamic vinegar
- 1 tablespoon olive oil
- Salt and freshly ground black pepper, to taste

Instructions:

1. In a bowl, add all the ingredients and toss to coat well.
2. Arrange the "Crisper Basket" in the pot of Ninja Foodi Grill.
3. Close the Ninja Foodi Grill with lid and select "Air Crisp".
4. Set the temperature to 350 degrees F to preheat.
5. Press "Start/Stop" to begin preheating.
6. When the display shows "Add Food" open the lid and place the Brussels sprouts into the "Crisper Basket".
7. Close the Ninja Foodi Grill with lid and set the time for 20 minutes.
8. Press "Start/Stop" to begin cooking.
9. When the cooking time is completed, press "Start/Stop" to stop cooking and open the lid.
10. Serve hot.

Nutritional Information per Serving:

Calories: 80 | Fat: 3.9g | Saturated Fat: 0.6g | Carbohydrates: 10.3g | Sugar: 2.5g | Protein: 3.9g

112. Seasoned Zucchini

⏰ Prep Time 10 m | ⏰ Cooking Time 10 m | 6 Servings

Ingredients:

- 4 large zucchinis, cut into slices
- ¼ cup olive oil
- ½ of onion, sliced
- ¾ teaspoon Italian seasoning
- ½ teaspoon garlic salt
- ¼ teaspoon seasoned salt

Instructions:

1. In a large bowl, mix together all the ingredients.
2. Arrange the greased "Crisper Basket" in the pot of Ninja Foodi Grill.
3. Close the Ninja Foodi Grill with lid and select "Air Crisp".
4. Set the temperature to 400 degrees F to preheat.
5. Press "Start/Stop" to begin preheating.
6. When the display shows "Add Food" open the lid and place the zucchini slices into the "Crisper Basket".
7. Close the Ninja Foodi Grill with lid and set the time for 10 minutes.
8. Press "Start/Stop" to begin cooking.
9. When the cooking time is completed, press "Start/Stop" to stop cooking and open the lid.
10. Serve hot.

Nutritional Information per Serving:

Calories: 106 | Fat: 8.9g | Saturated Fat: 1.3g | Carbohydrates: 6.9g | Sugar: 3.5g | Protein: 2.2g

113. Parmesan Asparagus

⏰ Prep Time 10 m | ⏰ Cooking Time 10 m | 3 Servings

Ingredients:

- 1 pound fresh asparagus, trimmed
- 1 tablespoon Parmesan cheese, grated
- 1 tablespoon butter, melted
- 1 teaspoon garlic powder
- Salt and freshly ground black pepper, to taste

Instructions:

1. In a bowl, mix together the asparagus, cheese, butter, garlic powder, salt, and black pepper.
2. Arrange the "Crisper Basket" in the pot of Ninja Foodi Grill.
3. Close the Ninja Foodi Grill with lid and select "Air Crisp".
4. Set the temperature to 400 degrees F to preheat.
5. Press "Start/Stop" to begin preheating.
6. When the display shows "Add Food" open the lid and place the veggie mixture into the "Crisper Basket".
7. Close the Ninja Foodi Grill with lid and set the time for 10 minutes.
8. Press "Start/Stop" to begin cooking.
9. When the cooking time is completed, press "Start/Stop" to stop cooking and open the lid.
10. Serve hot.

Nutritional Information per Serving:

Calories: 73 | Fat: 4.4g | Saturated Fat: 2.7g | Carbohydrates: 6.6g | Sugar: 3.1g | Protein: 4.2g

114. Stuffed Potatoes

⏰ Prep Time 15 m | ⏱ Cooking Time 26 m | 4 Servings

Ingredients:

- 4 potatoes, peeled
- 2-3 tablespoons canola oil
- 1 tablespoon butter
- ½ of brown onion, chopped
- 2 tablespoons fresh chives, chopped
- ½ cup Parmesan cheese, grated

Instructions:

1. Coat the potatoes with some oil.
2. Arrange the "Crisper Basket" in the pot of Ninja Foodi Grill.
3. Close the Ninja Foodi Grill with lid and select "Air Crisp".
4. Set the temperature to 390 degrees F to preheat.
5. Press "Start/Stop" to begin preheating.
6. When the display shows "Add Food" open the lid and place the potatoes into the "Crisper Basket".
7. Close the Ninja Foodi Grill with lid and set the time for 20 minutes.
8. Press "Start/Stop" to begin cooking.
9. Coat the potatoes twice with the remaining oil.
10. Meanwhile, in a frying pan, melt the butter over medium heat and sauté the onion for about 4-5 minutes.
11. Remove from the heat and transfer the onion into a bowl.
12. When cooking time is completed, press "Start/Stop" to stop cooking and open the lid.
13. Transfer the potatoes onto a platter.
14. Carefully cut each potato in half.
15. With a small scooper, scoop out the flesh from each half.
16. In the bowl of onion, add the potato flesh, chives, and half of cheese and stir to combine.
17. Stuff the potato halves with potato mixture evenly and sprinkle with the remaining cheese.
18. Again, arrange the potato halves in the "Crisper Basket".
19. Close the Ninja Foodi Grill with lid and select "Air Crisp".
20. Set the temperature to 390 degrees F for 6 minutes.
21. Press "Start/Stop" to begin cooking.
22. When cooking time is completed, press "Start/Stop" to stop cooking and open the lid.
23. Serve immediately.

Nutritional Information per Serving:

Calories: 276 | Fat: 12.5g | Saturated Fat: 3.6g | Carbohydrates: 34.8g | Sugar: 3.1g | Protein: 7.8g

115. Jacket Potatoes

⏰ Prep Time 10 m | ⏰ Cooking Time 15 m | 2 Servings

Ingredients:

- 2 potatoes
- 1 tablespoon mozzarella cheese, shredded
- 3 tablespoons sour cream
- 1 tablespoon butter, softened
- 1 teaspoon fresh chives, minced
- Salt and freshly ground black pepper, to taste

Instructions:

1. Arrange the greased "Crisper Basket" in the pot of Ninja Foodi Grill.
2. Close the Ninja Foodi Grill with lid and select "Air Crisp".
3. Set the temperature to 355 degrees F to preheat.
4. Press "Start/Stop" to begin preheating.
5. With a fork, prick the potatoes.
6. When the display shows "Add Food" open the lid and place the potatoes into the "Crisper Basket".
7. Close the Ninja Foodi Grill with lid and set the time for 15 minutes.
8. Press "Start/Stop" to begin cooking.
9. Meanwhile, in a bowl, add the remaining ingredients and mix until well combined.
10. When the cooking time is completed, press "Start/Stop" to stop cooking and open the lid.
11. Transfer the potatoes onto a platter.
12. Open potatoes from the center and stuff them with cheese mixture.
13. Serve immediately

Nutritional Information per Serving:
Calories: 277 | Fat: 12.2g | Saturated Fat: 7.6g | Carbohydrates: 34.8g | Sugar: 2.5g | Protein: 8.2g

116. Spicy Potatoes

⏰ Prep Time 15 m | ⏱ Cooking Time 25 m | 4 Servings

Ingredients:

- 2 cups water
- 6 russet potatoes, peeled and cubed
- ½ tablespoon extra-virgin olive oil
- ½ of onion, chopped
- 1 tablespoon fresh rosemary, chopped
- 1 garlic clove, minced
- 1 jalapeño pepper, chopped
- ½ teaspoon garam masala powder
- ¼ teaspoon ground cumin
- ¼ teaspoon red chili powder
- Salt and freshly ground black pepper, to taste

Instructions:

1. In a large bowl, add the water and potatoes and set aside for about 30 minutes.
2. Drain well and pat dry with the paper towels.
3. In a bowl, add the potatoes and oil and toss to coat well.
4. Arrange the "Crisper Basket" in the pot of Ninja Foodi Grill.
5. Close the Ninja Foodi Grill with lid and select "Air Crisp".
6. Set the temperature to 330 degrees F to preheat.
7. Press "Start/Stop" to begin preheating.
8. When the display shows "Add Food" open the lid and place the potato cubes into the "Crisper Basket".
9. Close the Ninja Foodi Grill with lid and set the time for 5 minutes.
10. Press "Start/Stop" to begin cooking.
11. When the cooking time is completed, press "Start/Stop" to stop cooking and open the lid.
12. Transfer the potatoes into a bowl.
13. Add the remaining ingredients and toss to coat well.
14. Again, place the potato cubes into the "Crisper Basket".
15. Close the Ninja Foodi Grill with lid and set the temperature to 390 degrees F for 25 minutes.
16. Close the Ninja Foodi Grill with lid and set the time for 5 minutes.
17. Press "Start/Stop" to begin cooking.
18. When the cooking time is completed, press "Start/Stop" to stop cooking and open the lid.
19. Serve hot.

Nutritional Information per Serving:

Calories: 274 | Fat: 2.3g | Saturated Fat: 0.4g | Carbohydrates: 52.6g | Sugar: 4.4g | Protein: 5.7g

117. Herbed Bell Peppers

⏰ Prep Time 10 m | ⏰ Cooking Time 8 m | 4 Servings

Ingredients:

- 1½ pounds bell peppers, seeded and cubed
- ½ teaspoon dried thyme, crushed
- ½ teaspoon dried savory, crushed
- Salt and freshly ground black pepper, to taste
- 2 teaspoons butter, melted

Instructions:

1. In a bowl, add the bell peppers, herbs, salt and black pepper and toss to coat well.
2. Arrange the greased "Crisper Basket" in the pot of Ninja Foodi Grill.
3. Close the Ninja Foodi Grill with lid and select "Air Crisp".
4. Set the temperature to 360 degrees F to preheat.
5. Press "Start/Stop" to begin preheating.
6. When the display shows "Add Food" open the lid and place the bell peppers into the "Crisper Basket".
7. Close the Ninja Foodi Grill with lid and set the time for 8 minutes.
8. Press "Start/Stop" to begin cooking.
9. When the cooking time is completed, press "Start/Stop" to stop cooking and open the lid.
10. Transfer the bell peppers into a bowl and drizzle with butter.
11. Serve immediately.

Nutritional Information per Serving:

Calories: 32 | Fat: 2.8 g | Saturated Fat: 1.2 g | Carbohydrates: 3.6g | Sugar: 2.3g | Protein: 0.5g

118. Marinated Tofu

⏰ Prep Time 15 m | ⏰ Cooking Time 20 m | 4 Servings

Ingredients:

- 2 tablespoons low-sodium soy sauce
- 2 tablespoon fish sauce
- 1 teaspoon sesame oil
- 12 ounces extra-firm tofu, drained and cubed into 1-inch size
- 1 teaspoon unsalted butter, melted

Instructions:

1. In a large bowl, place the soy sauce, fish sauce and sesame oil and mix until well combined.
2. Add the tofu cubes and toss to coat well.
3. Set aside to marinate for about 30 minutes, tossing occasionally.
4. Arrange the "Crisper Basket" in the pot of Ninja Foodi Grill.
5. Close the Ninja Foodi Grill with lid and select "Air Crisp".
6. Set the temperature to 355 degrees F to preheat. Press "Start/Stop" to begin preheating.
7. When the display shows "Add Food" open the lid and place the tofu cubes into the "Crisper Basket".
8. Drizzle the tofu cubes with the melted butter.
9. Close the Ninja Foodi Grill with lid and set the time for 25 minutes.
10. Press "Start/Stop" to begin cooking.
11. After 13 minutes of cooking, flip the tofu cubes.
12. When the cooking time is completed, press "Start/Stop" to stop cooking and open the lid.

Nutritional Information per Serving:

Calories: 102 | Fat: 7.1g | Saturated Fat: 1.2g | Carbohydrates: 2.5g | Sugar: 1.3g | Protein: 9.4g

APPETIZER & SNACK RECIPES

119. Buffalo Chicken Wings

Prep Time 15 m | Cooking Time 16 m | 5 Servings

Ingredients:

- 2 pounds frozen chicken wings, drums and flats separated
- 2 tablespoons olive oil
- 2 tablespoons Buffalo sauce
- ½ teaspoon red pepper flakes, crushed
- Salt, to taste

Instructions:

1. Coat the chicken wings with oi evenly.
2. Arrange the "Crisper Basket" in the pot of Ninja Foodi Grill.
3. Close the Ninja Foodi Grill with lid and select "Air Crisp".
4. Set the temperature to 390 degrees F to preheat.
5. Press "Start/Stop" to begin preheating.
6. When the display shows "Add Food" open the lid and place the chicken wings into the "Crisper Basket".
7. Close the Ninja Foodi Grill with lid and set the time for 16 minutes.
8. Press "Start/Stop" to begin cooking.
9. After 12 minutes of cooking, flip the wings and coat with barbecue sauce evenly.
10. Meanwhile, in a large bowl, add Buffalo sauce, red pepper flakes and salt and mix well.
11. When the cooking time is completed, press "Start/Stop" to stop cooking and open the lid.
12. Transfer the wings into a bowl.
13. Add the Buffalo sauce and toss to coat well.
14. Serve immediately.

Nutritional Information per Serving:

Calories: 394 | Fat: 19.1g | Saturated Fat: 4.5g | Carbohydrates: 0.2g | Sugar: 0.1g | Protein: 52.5g

120. BBQ Chicken Wings

⏰ Prep Time 15 m | ⏱ Cooking Time 9 m | 4 Servings

Ingredients:
- 2 pounds chicken wings
- 1 teaspoon olive oil
- 1 teaspoon smoked paprika
- 1 teaspoon garlic powder
- Salt and freshly ground black pepper, to taste
- ¼ cup barbecue sauce

Instructions:
1. In a large bowl, place chicken wings, smoked paprika, garlic powder, oil, salt, and black pepper and mix well.
2. Arrange the "Crisper Basket" in the pot of Ninja Foodi Grill.
3. Close the Ninja Foodi Grill with lid and select "Air Crisp".
4. Set the temperature to 360 degrees F to preheat.
5. Press "Start/Stop" to begin preheating.
6. When the display shows "Add Food" open the lid and place the chicken wings the "Crisper Basket" in a single layer.
7. Close the Ninja Foodi Grill with lid and select "Air Crisp".
8. Set the temperature to 360 degrees F for 19 minutes.
9. Press "Start/Stop" to begin cooking.
10. After 12 minutes of cooking, flip the wings and coat with barbecue sauce evenly.
11. When cooking time is completed, press "Start/Stop" to stop cooking and open the lid.
12. Serve immediately.

Nutritional Information per Serving:
Calories: 468|Fat: 18.1g|Saturated Fat: 4.8g|Carbohydrates: 6.5g|Sugar: 4.3g|Protein: 65.8g

121. Crispy Prawns

⏰ Prep Time 15 m | ⏱ Cooking Time 4 m | 8 Servings

Ingredients:
- 1 egg
- ½ pound nacho chips, crushed
- 18 prawns, peeled and deveined

Instructions:
1. In a shallow dish, crack the egg, and beat well.
2. Place the crushed nacho chips in another dish.
3. Now, dip the prawn into the beaten egg and then coat with the nacho chips.
4. Arrange the "Crisper Basket" in the pot of Ninja Foodi Grill.
5. Close the Ninja Foodi Grill with lid and select "Air Crisp".
6. Set the temperature to 355 degrees F to preheat.
7. Press "Start/Stop" to begin preheating.
8. When the display shows "Add Food" open the lid and place the prawns into the "Crisper Basket".
9. Close the Ninja Foodi Grill with lid and set the time for 8 minutes.
10. Press "Start/Stop" to begin cooking.
11. When the cooking time is completed, press "Start/Stop" to stop cooking and open the lid.
12. Serve hot.

Nutritional Information per Serving:
Calories: 212|Fat: 8.8g|Saturated Fat: 1.6g|Carbohydrates: 18.3g|Sugar: 1.1g|Protein: 14.3g

122. Crispy Shrimp

⏰ Prep Time 15 m | ⏰ Cooking Time 20 m | 4 Servings

Ingredients:
- ¼ cup all-purpose flour
- ½ cup mayonnaise
- ¼ cup sweet chili sauce
- 1 tablespoon Sriracha sauce
- 1 cup panko breadcrumbs
- 1 pound shrimp, peeled and deveined

Instructions:
1. In a shallow bowl, place the flour.
2. In a second bowl, mix together the mayonnaise, chili sauce, and Sriracha sauce.
3. In a third bowl, add the breadcrumbs.
4. Coat each shrimp with the flour, then dip into mayonnaise mixture and finally, coat with the breadcrumbs.
5. Arrange the greased "Crisper Basket" in the pot of Ninja Foodi Grill.
6. Close the Ninja Foodi Grill with lid and select "Air Crisp".
7. Set the temperature to 400 degrees F to preheat.
8. Press "Start/Stop" to begin preheating.
9. When the display shows "Add Food" open the lid and place half of the shrimp into the "Crisper Basket".
10. Close the Ninja Foodi Grill with lid and set the time for 10 minutes.
11. Press "Start/Stop" to begin cooking.
12. When the cooking time is completed, press "Start/Stop" to stop cooking and open the lid.
13. Transfer the shrimp onto a platter.
14. Repeat with the remaining shrimp.
15. Serve hot.

Nutritional Information per Serving:
Calories: 402 | Fat: 16.2g | Saturated Fat: 3.2g | Carbohydrates: 19.3g | Sugar: 2.4g | Protein: 27.7g

123. Bread Rolls

⏰ Prep Time 20 m | ⏱ Cooking Time 33 m | 8 Servings

Ingredients:

- 5 large potatoes, peeled
- 2 tablespoons vegetable oil, divided
- 2 small onions, finely chopped
- 2 green chilies, seeded and chopped
- 2 curry leaves
- ½ teaspoon ground turmeric
- Salt, to taste
- 8 bread slices, trimmed

Instructions:

1. In a pan of the boiling water, add the potatoes and cook for about 15-20 minutes.
2. Drain the potatoes well and with a potato masher, mash the potatoes.
3. In a skillet, heat 1 teaspoon of oil over a medium heat and sauté the onion for about 4-5 minutes.
4. Add the green chilies, curry leaves, and turmeric and sauté for about 1 minute.
5. Add in the mashed potatoes, and salt and mix well.
6. Remove from the heat and set aside to cool completely.
7. Make 8 equal-sized oval-shaped patties from the mixture.
8. Wet the bread slices completely with water.
9. With your hands, press each bread slices to remove the excess water.
10. Place 1 bread slice in your palm and place 1 patty in the center.
11. Roll the bread slice in a spindle shape and seal the edges to secure the filling.
12. Coat the roll with some oil.
13. Repeat with the remaining slices, filling and oil.
14. Arrange the "Crisper Basket" in the pot of Ninja Foodi Grill.
15. Close the Ninja Foodi Grill with lid and select "Air Crisp".
16. Set the temperature to 390 degrees F to preheat.
17. Press "Start/Stop" to begin preheating.
18. When the display shows "Add Food" open the lid and place the rolls into the "Crisper Basket".
19. Close the Ninja Foodi Grill with lid and set the time for 13 minutes.
20. Press "Start/Stop" to begin cooking.
21. When the cooking time is completed, press "Start/Stop" to stop cooking and open the lid.
22. Serve warm.

Nutritional Information per Serving:
Calories: 221 | Fat: 4g | Saturated Fat: 0.8g | Carbohydrates: 42.6g | Sugar: 3.8g | Protein: 4.8g

124. Beef Taquitos

⏲ Prep Time 15 m | ⏲ Cooking Time 8 m | 26 Servings

Ingredients:
- 6 corn tortillas
- 2 cups cooked beef, shredded
- ½ cup onion, chopped
- 1 cup pepper jack cheese, shredded
- Olive oil cooking spray

Instructions:
1. Arrange the tortillas onto a smooth surface.
2. Place the shredded meat over one corner of each tortilla, followed by onion and cheese.
3. Roll each tortilla to secure the filling and secure with toothpicks.
4. Spray each taquito with cooking spray evenly.
5. Arrange the taquitos onto the greased baking pan.
6. Arrange the "Crisper Basket" in the pot of Ninja Foodi Grill.
7. Close the Ninja Foodi Grill with lid and select "Air Crisp".
8. Set the temperature to 400 degrees F to preheat.
9. Press "Start/Stop" to begin preheating.
10. When the display shows "Add Food" open the lid and place the pan into the "Crisper Basket".
11. Close the Ninja Foodi Grill with lid and set the time for 8 minutes.
12. Press "Start/Stop" to begin cooking.
13. When the cooking time is completed, press "Start/Stop" to stop cooking and open the lid.
14. Serve warm.

Nutritional Information per Serving:
Calories: 228 | Fat: 9.6g | Saturated Fat: 4.8g | Carbohydrates: 12.3g | Sugar: 0.6g | Protein: 22.7g

125. Mixed Veggie Bites

⏰ Prep Time 15 m | ⏰ Cooking Time 10 m | 5 Servings

Ingredients:

- ¾ pound fresh spinach, blanched, drained and chopped
- ¼ of onion, chopped
- ½ of carrot, peeled and chopped
- 1 garlic clove, minced
- 1 American cheese slice, cut into tiny pieces
- 1 bread slice, toasted and processed into breadcrumbs
- ½ tablespoon corn flour
- ½ teaspoon red chili flakes
- Salt, to taste

Instructions:

1. In a bowl, add all the ingredients except breadcrumbs and mix until well combined.
2. Add the breadcrumbs and gently stir to combine.
3. Make 10 equal-sized balls from the mixture.
4. Arrange the "Crisper Basket" in the pot of Ninja Foodi Grill.
5. Close the Ninja Foodi Grill with lid and select "Air Crisp".
6. Set the temperature to 355 degrees F to preheat.
7. Press "Start/Stop" to begin preheating.
8. When the display shows "Add Food" open the lid and place the balls into the "Crisper Basket".
9. Close the Ninja Foodi Grill with lid and set the time for 10 minutes.
10. Press "Start/Stop" to begin cooking.
11. When the cooking time is completed, press "Start/Stop" to stop cooking and open the lid.
12. Serve warm.

Nutritional Information per Serving:
Calories: 43 | Fat: 1.4g | Saturated Fat: 0.7g | Carbohydrates: 5.6g | Sugar: 1.2g | Protein: 3.1g

126. Feta Tater Tots

⏰ Prep Time 15 m | ⏰ Cooking Time 25 m | 6 Servings

Ingredients:
- 2 pounds frozen tater tots
- ½ cup feta cheese, crumbled
- ½ cup tomato, chopped
- ¼ cup black olives, pitted and sliced
- ¼ cup red onion, chopped

Instructions:
1. Arrange the "Crisper Basket" in the pot of Ninja Foodi Grill.
2. Close the Ninja Foodi Grill with lid and select "Air Crisp".
3. Set the temperature to 450 degrees F to preheat.
4. Press "Start/Stop" to begin preheating.
5. When the display shows "Add Food" open the lid and place the tater tots into the "Crisper Basket".
6. Close the Ninja Foodi Grill with lid and set the time for 25 minutes.
7. Press "Start/Stop" to begin cooking.
8. After 15 minutes of cooking, transfer tots into a large bowl.
9. Add the feta cheese, tomatoes, olives and onion and toss to coat well.
10. Place the mixture into baking pan and arrange into the "Crisper Basket".
11. When the cooking time is completed, press "Start/Stop" to stop cooking and open the lid.
12. Serve warm.

Nutritional Information per Serving:
Calories: 332 | Fat: 17.7g | Saturated Fat: 5.6g | Carbohydrates: 37.9g | Sugar: 2g | Protein: 5.5g

127. Roasted Cashews

⏰ Prep Time 5 m | ⏰ Cooking Time 5 m | 6 Servings

Ingredients:
- 1½ cups raw cashew nuts
- 1 teaspoon butter, melted
- Salt and freshly ground black pepper, as needed

Instructions:
1. In a bowl, add all the ingredients and toss to coat well.
2. Arrange the "Crisper Basket" in the pot of Ninja Foodi Grill.
3. Close the Ninja Foodi Grill with lid and select "Air Crisp".
4. Set the temperature to 355 degrees F to preheat.
5. Press "Start/Stop" to begin preheating.
6. When the display shows "Add Food" open the lid and place the cashews into the "Crisper Basket".
7. Close the Ninja Foodi Grill with lid and set the time for 5 minutes.
8. Press "Start/Stop" to begin cooking.
9. Shake the cashews once halfway through.
10. When the cooking time is completed, press "Start/Stop" to stop cooking and open the lid.
11. Transfer the cashews onto a platter and set aside to cool before serving.

Nutritional Information per Serving:
Calories: 202 | Fat: 16.5g | Saturated Fat: 3.5g | Carbohydrates: 11.2g | Sugar: 1.7g | Protein: 5.3g

128. Tortilla Chips

⏰ Prep Time 10 m | ⏰ Cooking Time 3 m | 6 Servings

Ingredients:
- 8 corn tortillas, cut into triangle
- 1 tablespoon olive oil
- Salt, to taste

Instructions:
1. Coat the tortilla pieces with oil evenly.
2. Arrange the "Crisper Basket" in the pot of Ninja Foodi Grill.
3. Close the Ninja Foodi Grill with lid and select "Air Crisp".
4. Set the temperature to 390 degrees F to preheat.
5. Press "Start/Stop" to begin preheating.
6. When the display shows "Add Food" open the lid and place the tortilla pieces into the "Crisper Basket".
7. Close the Ninja Foodi Grill with lid and set the time for 3 minutes.
8. Press "Start/Stop" to begin cooking.
9. When the cooking time is completed, press "Start/Stop" to stop cooking and open the lid.
10. Serve warm.

Nutritional Information per Serving:
Calories: 90|Fat: 3.2g|Saturated Fat: 0.5g|Carbohydrates: 14.3g|Sugar: 0.3g|Protein: 1.8g

129. Apple Chips

⏰ Prep Time 10 m | ⏰ Cooking Time 8 m | 2 Servings

Ingredients:
- 1 apple, peeled, cored and thinly sliced
- 1 tablespoon sugar
- ½ teaspoon ground cinnamon
- Pinch of ground cardamom
- Pinch of ground ginger
- Pinch of salt

Instructions:
1. In a bowl, add all the ingredients and toss to coat well.
2. Arrange the greased "Crisper Basket" in the pot of Ninja Foodi Grill.
3. Close the Ninja Foodi Grill with lid and select "Air Crisp".
4. Set the temperature to 390 degrees F to preheat.
5. Press "Start/Stop" to begin preheating.
6. When the display shows "Add Food" open the lid and arrange the apple chips in "Crisper Basket".
7. Close the Ninja Foodi Grill with lid and set the time for 6 minutes.
8. Press "Start/Stop" to begin cooking.
9. When cooking time is completed, press "Start/Stop" to stop cooking and open the lid.
10. Set the apple chips aside to cool before serving.

Nutritional Information per Serving:
Calories: 82|Fat: 0.2g|Saturated Fat: 0g|Carbohydrates: 22g|Sugar: 17.6g|Protein: 0.3g

130. Spinach Chips

⏰ Prep Time 10 m | ⏰ Cooking Time 10 m | 3 Servings

Ingredients:
- 4 cups fresh baby spinach leaves
- 1 tablespoon olive oil
- 1/8 teaspoon cayenne pepper
- Salt and freshly ground black pepper, to taste

Instructions:
1. Arrange the "Crisper Basket" in the pot of Ninja Foodi Grill.
2. Close the Ninja Foodi Grill with lid and select "Air Crisp".
3. Set the temperature to 300 degrees to preheat.
4. Press "Start/Stop" to begin preheating.
5. In a bowl, add all the ingredients and toss to coat well.
6. When the display shows "Add Food" open the lid and place the spinach leaves into the "Crisper Basket" in a single layer.
7. Close the Ninja Foodi Grill with lid and set the time for 10 minutes.
8. Press "Start/Stop" to begin cooking.
9. When the cooking time is completed, press "Start/Stop" to stop cooking and open the lid.
10. Transfer the spinach chips onto a baking sheet for about 5-10 minutes.
11. Serve warm.

Nutritional Information per Serving:
Calories: 49|Fat: 4.8g|Saturated Fat: 0.7g|Carbohydrates: 1.5g|Sugar: 0.2g|Protein: 1.2g

131. French Fries

⏰ Prep Time 15 m | ⏰ Cooking Time 30 m | 4 Servings

Ingredients:
- 1 pound potatoes, peeled and cut into strips
- 3 tablespoons olive oil
- ½ teaspoon onion powder
- ½ teaspoon garlic powder
- 1 teaspoon paprika

Instructions:
1. In a large bowl of water, soak the potato strips for about 1 hour.
2. Drain the potato strips well and pat them dry with the paper towels.
3. In a large bowl, add the potato strips and the remaining ingredients and toss to coat well.
4. Arrange the "Crisper Basket" in the pot of Ninja Foodi Grill.
5. Close the Ninja Foodi Grill with lid and select "Air Crisp".
6. Set the temperature to 375 degrees F to preheat.
7. Press "Start/Stop" to begin preheating.
8. When the display shows "Add Food" open the lid and place the potato fries into the "Crisper Basket".
9. Close the Ninja Foodi Grill with lid and set the time for 30 minutes.
10. Press "Start/Stop" to begin cooking.
11. When the cooking time is completed, press "Start/Stop" to stop cooking and open the lid.
12. Serve warm.

Nutritional Information per Serving:
Calories: 172|Fat: 10.7g|Saturated Fat: 1.5g|Carbohydrates: 18.6g|Sugar: 1.6g|Protein: 2.1g

132. Zucchini Fries

⏱ Prep Time 10 m | ⏱ Cooking Time 20 m | 4 Servings

Ingredients:

- 1 pound zucchini, sliced into 2½-inch sticks
- Salt, to taste
- 2 tablespoons olive oil
- ¾ cup panko breadcrumbs

Instructions:

1. In a colander, add the zucchini and sprinkle with salt. Set aside for about 10 minutes.
2. Gently pat dry the zucchini sticks with the paper towels and coat with oil.
3. In a shallow dish, add the breadcrumbs.
4. Coat the zucchini sticks with breadcrumbs evenly.
5. Arrange the "Crisper Basket" in the pot of Ninja Foodi Grill.
6. Close the Ninja Foodi Grill with lid and select "Air Crisp".
7. Set the temperature to 390 degrees F to preheat.
8. Press "Start/Stop" to begin preheating.
9. When the display shows "Add Food" open the lid and place half of the zucchini fries into the "Crisper Basket".
10. Close the Ninja Foodi Grill with lid and set the time for 10 minutes.
11. Press "Start/Stop" to begin cooking.
12. When the cooking time is completed, press "Start/Stop" to stop cooking and open the lid.
13. Transfer the fries onto a platter.
14. Repeat with the remaining fries.
15. Serve warm.

Nutritional Information per Serving:

Calories: 78 | Fat: 8.6g | Saturated Fat: 1.6g | Carbohydrates: 6.9g | Sugar: 2g | Protein: 1.9g

133. Mozzarella Sticks

⏰ Prep Time 15 m | ⏰ Cooking Time 12 m | 3 Servings

Ingredients:

- 3 tablespoons white flour
- 2 eggs
- 3 tablespoons milk
- ½ cup plain breadcrumbs
- ½ pound mozzarella cheese block, cut into 3x½-inch sticks

Instructions:

1. In a shallow dish, place the flour.
2. In a second shallow dish, add eggs and milk and beat well.
3. In a third shallow dish, place the breadcrumbs.
4. Coat the Mozzarella sticks with flour, then dip into egg mixture and finally, coat with the breadcrumbs.
5. Arrange the Mozzarella sticks onto a cookie sheet and freeze for about 1-2 hours.
6. Arrange the "Crisper Basket" in the pot of Ninja Foodi Grill.
7. Close the Ninja Foodi Grill with lid and select "Air Crisp".
8. Set the temperature to 400 degrees F to preheat.
9. Press "Start/Stop" to begin preheating.
10. When the display shows "Add Food" open the lid and place the mozzarella sticks into the "Crisper Basket".
11. Close the Ninja Foodi Grill with lid and set the time for 12 minutes.
12. Press "Start/Stop" to begin cooking.
13. When the cooking time is completed, press "Start/Stop" to stop cooking and open the lid.
14. Serve warm.

Nutritional Information per Serving:
Calories: 162 | Fat: 5.1g | Saturated Fat: 1.8g | Carbohydrates: 20.1g | Sugar: 2.1g | Protein: 8.7g

134. Chicken Nuggets

⏰ Prep Time 15 m | ⏰ Cooking Time 10 m | 5 Servings

Ingredients:

- ½ of zucchini, chopped roughly
- ½ of carrot, peeled and chopped roughly
- 14 ounces boneless, skinless chicken breasts, cut into chunks
- ½ tablespoon mustard powder
- 1 tablespoon garlic powder
- 1 tablespoon onion powder
- Salt and freshly ground black pepper, to taste
- 1 cup all-purpose flour
- 2 tablespoons milk
- 1 egg
- 1 cup panko breadcrumbs

Instructions:

1. In a food processor, add zucchini and carrot and pulse until chopped finely.
2. Add the chicken, mustard powder, garlic powder, onion powder, salt and black pepper and pulse until just combined.
3. Make equal-sized nuggets from the mixture.
4. In a shallow dish, place the flour.
5. In a second shallow dish, beat the milk and egg.
6. In a third shallow dish, place the breadcrumbs.
7. Coat the nuggets with flour, then dip into egg mixture and finally, coat with the breadcrumbs.
8. Arrange the "Crisper Basket" in the pot of Ninja Foodi Ninja Foodi Grill with lid and select "Air Crisp".
9. Set the temperature to 390 degrees F to preheat.
10. Press "Start/Stop" to begin preheating.
11. When the display shows "Add Food" open the lid and place the nuggets into the "Crisper Basket" in a single layer.
12. Close the Ninja Foodi Grill with lid and set the time for 10 minutes.
13. Press "Start/Stop" to begin cooking.
14. When the cooking time is completed, press "Start/Stop" to stop cooking and open the lid.
15. Serve warm.

Nutritional Information per Serving:

Calories: 357 | Fat: 9g | Saturated Fat: 2.6g | Carbohydrates: 26.7g | Sugar: 2.1g | Protein: 28.4g

135. Bacon Croquettes

⏰ Prep Time 8 m | ⏰ Cooking Time 15 m | 8 Servings

Ingredients:

- 1 pound thin bacon slices
- 1 pound sharp cheddar cheese block, cut into 1-inch rectangular pieces
- 1 cup all-purpose flour
- 3 eggs
- 1 cup breadcrumbs
- Salt, as require
- ¼ cup olive oil

Instructions:

1. Wrap 2 bacon slices around 1 piece of cheddar cheese, covering completely.
2. Repeat with the remaining bacon and cheese pieces.
3. Arrange the croquettes in a baking pan and freeze for about 5 minutes.
4. In a shallow dish, place the flour.
5. In a second shallow dish, crack the eggs and beat well.
6. In a third shallow dish, mix together the breadcrumbs, salt, and oil.
7. Coat the croquettes with flour, then dip into beaten eggs and finally coat with the breadcrumbs mixture.
8. Arrange the "Crisper Basket" in the pot of Ninja Foodi Grill.
9. Close the Ninja Foodi Grill with lid and select "Air Crisp".
10. Set the temperature to 390 degrees F to preheat.
11. Press "Start/Stop" to begin preheating.
12. When the display shows "Add Food" open the lid and place the croquettes into the "Crisper Basket" in a single layer.
13. Close the Ninja Foodi Grill with lid and set the time for 8 minutes
14. Press "Start/Stop" to begin cooking.
15. When the cooking time is completed, press "Start/Stop" to stop cooking and open the lid and
16. Serve warm.

Nutritional Information per Serving:

Calories: 591 | Fat: 43.5g | Saturated Fat: 13.8g | Carbohydrates: 23.4g | Sugar: 1.3g | Protein: 26.6g

136. Potato Croquettes

⏰ Prep Time 15 m | ⏰ Cooking Time 23 m | 4 Servings

Ingredients:

- 2 medium Russet potatoes, peeled and cubed
- 2 tablespoons all-purpose flour
- ½ cup Parmesan cheese, grated
- 1 egg yolk
- 2 tablespoons chives, minced
- Pinch of ground nutmeg
- Salt and freshly ground black pepper, to taste
- 2 eggs
- ½ cup breadcrumbs
- 2 tablespoons vegetable oil

Instructions:

1. In a pan of boiling water, add potatoes and cook for about 15 minutes.
2. Drain the potatoes well and transfer into a large bowl.
3. With a potato masher, mash the potatoes and set aside to cool completely.
4. In the same bowl of mashed potatoes, add in the flour, Parmesan cheese, egg yolk, chives, nutmeg, salt, and black pepper and mix until well combined.
5. Make small equal-sized balls from the mixture.
6. Now, roll each ball into a cylinder shape.
7. In a shallow dish, crack the eggs and beat well.
8. In another dish, mix together the breadcrumbs and oil.
9. Dip the croquettes in egg mixture and then coat with the breadcrumbs mixture.
10. Arrange the "Crisper Basket" in the pot of Ninja Foodi Grill.
11. Close the Ninja Foodi Grill with lid and select "Air Crisp".
12. Set the temperature to 390 degrees F to preheat.
13. Press "Start/Stop" to begin preheating.
14. When the display shows "Add Food" open the lid and place the croquettes into the "Crisper Basket" in a single layer.
15. Close the Ninja Foodi Grill with lid and set the time for 8 minutes.
16. Press "Start/Stop" to begin cooking.
17. When the cooking time is completed, press "Start/Stop" to stop cooking and open the lid.
18. Serve warm.

Nutritional Information per Serving:
Calories: 283 | Fat: 13.4g | Saturated Fat: 3.8g | Carbohydrates: 29.9g | Sugar: 2.3g | Protein: 11.5g

137. Broccoli Bites

⏰ Prep Time 15 m | ⏰ Cooking Time 12 m | 6 Servings

Ingredients:

- 2 cups broccoli florets
- 2 eggs, beaten
- 1¼ cups cheddar cheese, grated
- ¼ cup Parmesan cheese, grated
- 1¼ cups panko breadcrumbs
- Salt and freshly ground black pepper, to taste

Instructions:

1. In a food processor, add the broccoli and pulse until crumbed finely.
2. In a large bowl, place the broccoli and remaining ingredients and mix until well combined.
3. Make small equal-sized balls from mixture.
4. Arrange the balls onto a parchment-lined baking sheet and refrigerate for at least 30 minutes.
5. Arrange the "Crisper Basket" in the pot of Ninja Foodi Grill.
6. Close the Ninja Foodi Grill with lid and select "Air Crisp".
7. Set the temperature to 350 degrees to preheat.
8. Press "Start/Stop" to begin preheating.
9. When the display shows "Add Food" open the lid and place the broccoli balls into the "Crisper Basket" in a single layer.
10. Close the Ninja Foodi Grill with lid and set the time for 12 minutes.
11. When the cooking time is completed, press "Start/Stop" to stop cooking and open the lid.
12. Serve warm.

Nutritional Information per Serving:

Calories: 247 | Fat: 13.6g | Saturated Fat: 7.7g | Carbohydrates: 6.5g | Sugar: 0.8g | Protein: 13.2g

138. Cauliflower Poppers

⏰ Prep Time 10 m | ⏰ Cooking Time 20 m | 6 Servings

Ingredients:
- 3 tablespoons olive oil
- ½ teaspoon paprika
- ½ teaspoon cayenne pepper
- ½ teaspoon ground cumin
- ¼ teaspoon ground turmeric
- Salt and freshly ground black pepper, to taste
- 1 medium head cauliflower, cut into florets

Instructions:
1. In a bowl, place all ingredients and toss to coat well.
2. Place the cauliflower mixture in the greased baking pan.
3. Arrange the "Crisper Basket" in the pot of Ninja Foodi Grill.
4. Close the Ninja Foodi Grill with lid and select "Bake".
5. Set the temperature to 450 degrees F to preheat.
6. Press "Start/Stop" to begin preheating.
7. When the display shows "Add Food" open the lid and place the pan into the "Crisper Basket".
8. Close the Ninja Foodi Grill with lid and set the time for 20 minutes.
9. Press "Start/Stop" to begin cooking.
10. Stir the dip once halfway through.
11. When cooking time is completed, press "Start/Stop" to stop cooking and open the lid.
12. Serve warm.

Nutritional Information per Serving:
Calories: 73 | Fat: 7.1g | Saturated Fat: 1g | Carbohydrates: 2.7g | Sugar: 1.1g | Protein: 1g

139. Spinach Dip

⏲ Prep Time 15 m | ⏲ Cooking Time 35 m | 8 Servings

Ingredients:

- 1 (8-ounce) package cream cheese, softened
- 1 cup mayonnaise
- 1 cup Parmesan cheese, grated
- 1 cup frozen spinach, thawed and squeezed
- 1/3 cup water chestnuts, drained and chopped
- ½ cup onion, minced
- ¼ teaspoon garlic powder
- Freshly ground black pepper, to taste

Instructions:

1. In a bowl, add all the ingredients and mix until well combined.
2. Transfer the mixture into a baking pan. and spread in an even layer.
3. Arrange the "Crisper Basket" in the pot of Ninja Foodi Grill.
4. Close the Ninja Foodi Grill with lid and select "Bake".
5. Set the temperature to 300 degrees F to preheat.
6. Press "Start/Stop" to begin preheating.
7. When the display shows "Add Food" open the lid and place the pan into the "Crisper Basket".
8. Close the Ninja Foodi Grill with lid and set the time for 30 minutes.
9. Press "Start/Stop" to begin cooking.
10. Stir the dip once halfway through.
11. When cooking time is completed, press "Start/Stop" to stop cooking and open the lid.
12. Serve hot.

Nutritional Information per Serving:
Calories: 258 | Fat: 22.1g | Saturated Fat: 8.9g | Carbohydrates: 9.4g | Sugar: 2.3g | Protein: 6.7g

140. Onion Dip

⏰ Prep Time 10 m | ⏰ Cooking Time 35 m | 10 Servings

Ingredients:

- 2/3 cup onion, chopped
- 1 cup cheddar Jack cheese, shredded
- ½ cup Swiss cheese, shredded
- ¼ cup Parmesan cheese, shredded
- 2/3 cup whipped salad dressing
- ½ cup milk
- Salt, to taste

Instructions:

1. In a large bowl, add all the ingredients and mix well.
2. Transfer the mixture into a baking pan. and spread in an even layer.
3. Arrange the "Crisper Basket" in the pot of Ninja Foodi Grill.
4. Close the Ninja Foodi Grill with lid and select "Bake".
5. Set the temperature to 375 degrees F to preheat.
6. Press "Start/Stop" to begin preheating.
7. When the display shows "Add Food" open the lid and place the pan into the "Crisper Basket".
8. Close the Ninja Foodi Grill with lid and set the time for 45 minutes.
9. Press "Start/Stop" to begin cooking.
10. When cooking time is completed, press "Start/Stop" to stop cooking and open the lid.
11. Serve hot.

Nutritional Information per Serving:
Calories: 87 | Fat: 6 g | Saturated Fat: 3.5 g | Carbohydrates: 2.3 g | Sugar: 1.1 g | Protein: 5.1 g

DESSERT RECIPES

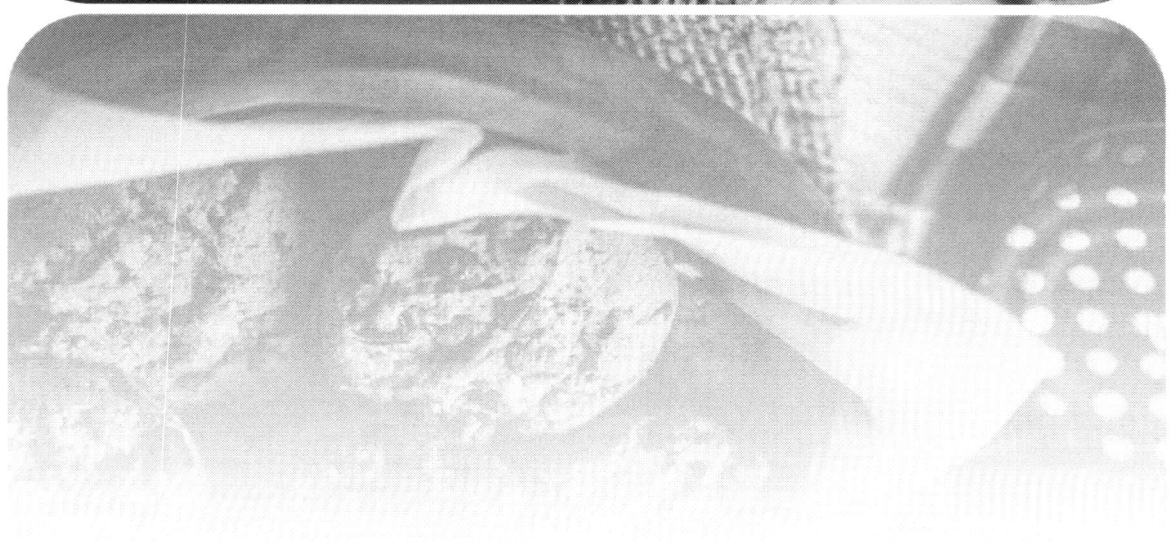

141. Lava Cake

⏰ Prep Time 15 m | ⏰ Cooking Time 12 m | 4 Servings

Ingredients:

- 2/3 cup chocolate chips
- ½ cup unsalted butter
- 2 large eggs
- 2 large egg yolks
- 1 cup confectioners' sugar
- 1 teaspoon peppermint extract
- 1/3 cup all-purpose flour plus more for dusting
- 2 tablespoons powdered sugar
- ¼ cup fresh raspberries

Instructions:

1. In a microwave-safe bowl, place the chocolate chips and butter and microwave on High for about 30 seconds.
2. Remove the bowl from microwave and stir the mixture well.
3. Add the eggs, egg yolks and confectioners' Sugar: and beat until well combined.
4. Add the flour and gently stir to combine.
5. Grease 4 ramekins and dust each with a little flour.
6. Place the chocolate mixture into the prepared ramekins evenly.
7. Arrange the "Crisper Basket" in the pot of Ninja Foodi Grill.
8. Close the Ninja Foodi Grill with lid and select "Air Crisp".
9. Set the temperature to 375 degrees F to preheat.
10. Press "Start/Stop" to begin preheating.
11. When the display shows "Add Food" open the lid and place the ramekins into the "Crisper Basket".
12. Close the Ninja Foodi Grill with lid and set the time for 12 minutes.
13. Press "Start/Stop" to begin cooking.
14. When cooking time is completed, press "Start/Stop" to stop cooking and open the lid.
15. Transfer the ramekins onto a wire rack for about 5 minutes.
16. Carefully run a knife around the sides of each ramekin many times to loosen the cake.
17. Carefully invert each cake onto a dessert plate and dust with powdered Sugar:.
18. Garnish with raspberries and serve immediately.

Nutritional Information per Serving:

Calories: 596 | Fat: 36.2g | Saturated Fat: 22g | Carbohydrates: 60.1g | Sugar: 19.1g | Protein: 8.1g

142. Butter Cake

⏲ Prep Time 15 m | ⏲ Cooking Time 15 m | 6 Servings

Ingredients:

- 3 ounces butter, softened
- ½ cup caster sugar
- 1 egg
- 1 1/3 cups plain flour, sifted
- Pinch of salt
- ½ cup milk
- 1 tablespoon icing sugar

Instructions:

1. In a bowl, add the butter, and sugar and whisk until light and creamy.
2. Add the egg and whisk until smooth and fluffy.
3. Add the flour, and salt and mix well alternately with the milk.
4. Grease a small Bundt cake pan.
5. Place mixture into the prepared cake pan evenly.
6. Arrange the "Crisper Basket" in the pot of Ninja Foodi Grill.
7. Close the Ninja Foodi Grill with lid and select "Air Crisp".
8. Set the temperature to 350 degrees F to preheat.
9. Press "Start/Stop" to begin preheating.
10. When the display shows "Add Food" open the lid and place the pan into the "Crisper Basket".
11. Close the Ninja Foodi Grill with lid and set the time for 15 minutes.
12. Press "Start/Stop" to begin cooking.
13. When the cooking time is completed, press "Start/Stop" to stop cooking and open the lid.
14. Place the cake pan onto a wire rack to cool for about 10 minutes.
15. Carefully invert the cake onto wire rack to completely cool before slicing.
16. Dust the cake with icing sugar and cut into desired sized slices.

Nutritional Information per Serving:
Calories: 291 | Fat: 12.9g | Saturated Fat: 7.8g | Carbohydrates: 40.3g | Sugar: 19g | Protein: 4.6g

143. Chocolate Brownie Cake

⏰ Prep Time 15 m | ⏰ Cooking Time 35 m | 6 Servings

Ingredients:
- ½ cup dark chocolate chips
- ½ cup butter
- 3 eggs
- ¼ cup sugar
- 1 teaspoon vanilla extract

Instructions:
1. In a microwave-safe bowl, add the chocolate chips and butter and microwave for about 1 minute, stirring after every 20 seconds.
2. Remove from the microwave and stir well.
3. Arrange the "Crisper Basket" in the pot of Ninja Foodi Grill.
4. Close the Ninja Foodi Grill with lid and select "Air Crisp".
5. Set the temperature to 350 degrees F to preheat.
6. Press "Start/Stop" to begin preheating.
7. In a bowl, add the eggs, sugar and vanilla extract and blend until light and frothy.
8. Slowly add the chocolate mixture and beat again until well combined.
9. Place the mixture into a lightly greased springform pan.
10. When the display shows "Add Food" open the lid and place the springform pan into the "Crisper Basket".
11. Close the Ninja Foodi Grill with lid and set the time for 35 minutes.
12. Press "Start/Stop" to begin cooking.
13. When the cooking time is completed, press "Start/Stop" to stop cooking and open the lid.
14. Place the pan onto a wire rack to cool for about 10 minutes.
15. Carefully invert the cake onto the wire rack to cool completely.
16. Cut into desired sized slices and serve.
17. Place the pan onto a wire rack to cool for about 10 minutes.

Nutritional Information per Serving:
Calories: 247 | Fat: 20.2g | Saturated Fat: 12.1g | Carbohydrates: 15.3g | Sugar: 13.9g | Protein: 3.6g

144. Mini Cheesecakes

⏰ Prep Time 10 m | ⏰ Cooking Time 10 m | 2 Servings

Ingredients:

- ¾ cup Erythritol
- 2 eggs
- 1 teaspoon vanilla extract
- ½ teaspoon fresh lemon juice
- 16 ounces cream cheese, softened
- 2 tablespoon sour cream

Instructions:

1. In a blender, add the Erythritol, eggs, vanilla extract and lemon juice and pulse until smooth.
2. Add the cream cheese and sour cream and pulse until smooth.
3. Place the mixture into 2 (4-inch) springform pans evenly.
4. Arrange the "Crisper Basket" in the pot of Ninja Foodi Grill.
5. Close the Ninja Foodi Grill with lid and select "Air Crisp".
6. Set the temperature to 350 degrees F to preheat.
7. Press "Start/Stop" to begin preheating.
8. When the display shows "Add Food" open the lid and place the pans into the "Crisper Basket".
9. Close the Ninja Foodi Grill with lid and set the time for 10 minutes.
10. Press "Start/Stop" to begin cooking.
11. When cooking time is completed, press "Start/Stop" to stop cooking and open the lid.
12. Place the pans onto a wire rack to cool completely.
13. Refrigerate overnight before serving.

Nutritional Information per Serving:

Calories: 886 | Fat: 86g | Saturated Fat: 52.8g | Carbohydrates: 7.2g | Sugar: 1.1g | Protein: 23.1g

145. Vanilla Cheesecake

⏰ Prep Time 15 m | ⏰ Cooking Time 14 m | 6 Servings

Ingredients:

- 1 cup honey graham cracker crumbs
- 2 tablespoons unsalted butter, softened
- 1 pound cream cheese, softened
- ½ cup sugar
- 2 large eggs
- ½ teaspoon vanilla extract

Instructions:

1. Line a round baking pan with parchment paper.
2. For crust: in a bowl, add the graham cracker crumbs, and butter.
3. Place the crust into baking pan and press to smooth.
4. Arrange the "Crisper Basket" in the pot of Ninja Foodi Grill.
5. Close the Ninja Foodi Grill with lid and select "Air Crisp".
6. Set the temperature to 350 degrees F to preheat.
7. Press "Start/Stop" to begin preheating.
8. When the display shows "Add Food" open the lid and place the pan into the "Crisper Basket".
9. Close the Ninja Foodi Grill with lid and set the time for 4 minutes.
10. Press "Start/Stop" to begin cooking.
11. When cooking time is completed, press "Start/Stop" to stop cooking and open the lid.
12. Place the crust aside to cool for about 10 minutes.
13. Meanwhile, in a bowl, add the cream cheese, and sugar and whisk until smooth.
14. Place the eggs, one at a time and whisk until mixture becomes creamy.
15. Add the vanilla extract and mix well.
16. Place the cream cheese mixture evenly over the crust.
17. Arrange the "Crisper Basket" in the pot of Ninja Foodi Grill.
18. Close the Ninja Foodi Grill with lid and select "Air Crisp".
19. Set the temperature to 350 degrees F to preheat.
20. Press "Start/Stop" to begin preheating.
21. When the display shows "Add Food" open the lid and place the pan into the "Crisper Basket".
22. Close the Ninja Foodi Grill with lid and set the time for 10 minutes.
23. Press "Start/Stop" to begin cooking.
24. When cooking time is completed, press "Start/Stop" to stop cooking and open the lid.
25. Place the pan onto a wire rack to cool completely.
26. Refrigerate overnight before serving.

Nutritional Information per Serving:
Calories: 470 | Fat: 33.9g | Saturated Fat: 20.6g | Carbohydrates: 34.9g | Sugar: 22g | Protein: 9.4

146. Pumpkin Pie

⏰ Prep Time 10 m | ⏰ Cooking Time 20 m | 6 Servings

Ingredients:

- 1 package pie crust
- 3 eggs
- 1 (15-ounce) can pumpkin
- ¾ cup brown sugar
- 1 teaspoon ground cinnamon
- 1 teaspoon ground ginger
- 1 teaspoon ground nutmeg
- ½ teaspoon ground cloves
- 1 cup light cream

Instructions:

1. Arrange the pie crust into a tart pan and press to smooth.
2. In a large bowl, add the eggs, pumpkin, brown Sugar: and spices and beat until well combined.
3. Add the light cream and stir to combine.
4. Place the mixture over the crust evenly.
5. Arrange the "Crisper Basket" in the pot of Ninja Foodi Grill.
6. Close the Ninja Foodi Grill with lid and select "Air Crisp".
7. Set the temperature to 320 degrees F to preheat.
8. Press "Start/Stop" to begin preheating.
9. When the display shows "Add Food" open the lid and place the pan into the "Crisper Basket".
10. Close the Ninja Foodi Grill with lid and set the time for 10 minutes.
11. Press "Start/Stop" to begin cooking.
12. After 10 minutes of cooking, set the temperature to 300 degrees F for 10 minutes.
13. When cooking time is completed, press "Start/Stop" to stop cooking and open the lid.
14. Place the pie pan onto a wire rack to cool for about 10-15 minutes before serving.

Nutritional Information per Serving:
Calories: 261 | Fat: 12.5g | Saturated Fat: 5.6g | Carbohydrates: 34.9g | Sugar: 26g | Protein: 4.7g

147. Pecan Pie

⏰ Prep Time 15 m | ⏰ Cooking Time 35 m | 5 Servings

Ingredients:
- ¾ cup brown sugar
- ¼ cup caster sugar
- 1/3 cup butter, melted
- 2 large eggs
- 1¾ tablespoons flour
- 1 tablespoon milk
- 1 teaspoon vanilla extract
- 1 cup pecan halves
- 1 frozen pie crust, thawed

Instructions:
1. In a large bowl, mix together the sugars and butter.
2. Add the eggs and whisk until foamy.
3. Add the flour, milk, and vanilla extract and whisk until well combined.
4. Fold in the pecan halves.
5. Grease a pie pan.
6. Arrange the crust in the bottom of prepared pie pan.
7. Place the pecan mixture over the crust evenly.
8. Arrange the "Crisper Basket" in the pot of Ninja Foodi Grill.
9. Close the Ninja Foodi Grill with lid and select "Air Crisp".
10. Set the temperature to 300 degrees F to preheat.
11. Press "Start/Stop" to begin preheating.
12. When the display shows "Add Food" open the lid and place the pan into the "Crisper Basket".
13. Close the Ninja Foodi Grill with lid and set the time for 22 minutes.
14. Press "Start/Stop" to begin cooking.
15. After 22 minutes of cooking, set the temperature to 385 degrees F for 13 minutes.
16. When cooking time is completed, press "Start/Stop" to stop cooking and open the lid.
17. Place the pie pan onto a wire rack to cool for about 10-15 minutes before serving.

Nutritional Information per Serving:
Calories: 501 | Fat: 35g | Saturated Fat: 10.8g | Carbohydrates: 44.7g | Sugar: 36.7g | Protein: 6.2g

148. Plum Crisps

⏱ Prep Time 15 m | ⏱ Cooking Time 40 m | 2 Servings

Ingredients:

- 1½ cups plums, pitted and sliced
- ¼ cup sugar, divided
- 1½ teaspoons cornstarch
- 3 tablespoons flour
- ¼ teaspoon ground cinnamon
- Pinch of salt
- 1½ tablespoons cold butter, chopped
- 3 tablespoons rolled oats

Instructions:

1. In a bowl, place plum slices, 1 teaspoon of Sugar: and cornstarch and toss to coat well.
2. Divide the plum mixture into lightly greased 2 (8-ounce) ramekins.
3. In a bowl, mix together the flour, remaining sugar, cinnamon and salt.
4. With a pastry blender, cut in butter until a crumbly mixture forms.
5. Add the oats and gently stir to combine.
6. Place the oat mixture over plum slices into each ramekin.
7. Arrange the "Crisper Basket" in the pot of Ninja Foodi Grill.
8. Close the Ninja Foodi Grill with lid and select "Bake".
9. Set the temperature to 350 degrees F to preheat.
10. Press "Start/Stop" to begin preheating.
11. When the display shows "Add Food" open the lid and place the ramekins into the "Crisper Basket".
12. Close the Ninja Foodi Grill with lid and set the time for 40 minutes.
13. Press "Start/Stop" to begin cooking.
14. When the cooking time is completed, press "Start/Stop" to stop cooking and open the lid.
15. Place the ramekins onto a wire rack to cool for about 10 minutes.
16. Serve warm.

Nutritional Information per Serving:

Calories: 273 | Fat: 9.4g | Saturated Fat: 5.6g | Carbohydrates: 47.2g | Sugar: 30.4g | Protein: 2.7g

149. Cherry Clafoutis

⏰ Prep Time 15 m | ⏰ Cooking Time 25 m | 4 Servings

Ingredients:

- 1½ cups fresh cherries, pitted
- 3 tablespoons vodka
- ¼ cup flour
- 2 tablespoons sugar
- Pinch of salt
- ½ cup sour cream
- 1 egg
- 1 tablespoon butter
- ¼ cup powdered sugar

Instructions:

1. In a bowl, mix together the cherries and vodka.
2. In another bowl, place the flour, sugar and salt and mix well.
3. Add the sour cream and egg and mix until a smooth dough forms.
4. Place the flour mixture into a greased cake pan evenly.
5. Spread cherry mixture over the dough evenly.
6. Place the butter on top in the form of dots.
7. Arrange the "Crisper Basket" in the pot of Ninja Foodi Grill.
8. Close the Ninja Foodi Grill with lid and select "Air Crisp".
9. Set the temperature to 355 degrees F to preheat.
10. Press "Start/Stop" to begin preheating.
11. When the display shows "Add Food" open the lid and place the cake pan into the "Crisper Basket".
12. Close the Ninja Foodi Grill with lid and set the time for 25 minutes.
13. Press "Start/Stop" to begin cooking.
14. When the cooking time is completed, press "Start/Stop" to stop cooking and open the lid.
15. Transfer the cake pan onto a wire rack to cool for about 10 minutes.
16. Now, invert the Clafoutis onto a platter and sprinkle with powdered sugar.
17. Cut the Clafoutis into desired-sized slices and serve warm.

Nutritional Information per Serving:

Calories: 241 | Fat: 10.1g | Saturated 5.9g | Carbohydrates: 29g | Sugar: 20.6g | Protein: 3.9g

150. Lemon Mousse

⏰ Prep Time 10 m | ⏰ Cooking Time 12 m | 2 Servings

Ingredients:
- 4 ounces cream cheese, softened
- ½ cup heavy cream
- 2 tablespoons fresh lemon juice
- 2 tablespoons honey
- 2 pinches of salt

Instructions:
1. In a bowl, add all the ingredients and mix until well combined.
2. Transfer the mixture into 2 ramekins.
3. Arrange the "Crisper Basket" in the pot of Ninja Foodi Grill.
4. Close the Ninja Foodi Grill with lid and select "Bake".
5. Set the temperature to 350 degrees F to preheat.
6. Press "Start/Stop" to begin preheating.
7. When the display shows "Add Food" open the lid and place the ramekins into the "Crisper Basket".
8. Close the Ninja Foodi Grill with lid and set the time for 12 minutes.
9. Press "Start/Stop" to begin cooking.
10. When the cooking time is completed, press "Start/Stop" to stop cooking and open the lid.
11. Place the ramekins onto a wire rack to cool.
12. Refrigerate for at least 3 hours before serving.

Nutritional Information per Serving:
Calories: 369 | Fat: 31g | Saturated Fat: 19.5g | Carbohydrates: 20g | Sugar: 17.7g | Protein: 5.1g

151. Apple Bread Pudding

⏰ Prep Time 15 m | ⏰ Cooking Time 12 m | 3 Servings

Ingredients:

- 1 cup milk
- 1 egg
- 1 tablespoon brown sugar
- ½ teaspoon ground cinnamon
- ¼ teaspoon vanilla extract
- 2 tablespoons raisins, soaked in hot water for about 15 minutes
- 2 bread slices, cut into small cubes
- 1 tablespoon chocolate chips
- 1 tablespoon sugar

Instructions:

1. In a bowl, mix together the milk, egg, brown sugar, cinnamon, and vanilla extract.
2. Stir in the raisins.
3. In a baking pan, spread the bread cubes and top with the milk mixture evenly.
4. Refrigerate for about 15-20 minutes, tossing occasionally.
5. Arrange the "Crisper Basket" in the pot of Ninja Foodi Grill.
6. Close the Ninja Foodi Grill with lid and select "Air Crisp".
7. Set the temperature to 375 degrees F to preheat.
8. Press "Start/Stop" to begin preheating.
9. When the display shows "Add Food" open the lid and place the pan into the "Crisper Basket".
10. Close the Ninja Foodi Grill with lid and set the time for 12 minutes.
11. Press "Start/Stop" to begin cooking.
12. When cooking time is completed, press "Start/Stop" to stop cooking and open the lid.
13. Serve warm.

Nutritional Information per Serving:
Calories: 143 | Fat: 4.4g | Saturated Fat: 2.2g | Carbohydrates: 21.3g | Sugar: 16.4g | Protein: 5.5g

152. Chocolate Pudding

⏰ Prep Time 15 m | ⏰ Cooking Time 14 m | 4 Servings

Ingredients:

- ½ cup butter
- 2/3 cup dark chocolate, chopped
- ¼ cup caster sugar
- 2 medium eggs
- 2 teaspoons fresh orange rind, finely grated
- ¼ cup fresh orange juice
- 2 tablespoons self-rising flour

Instructions:

1. In a microwave-safe bowl, add the butter, and chocolate and microwave on high for about 2 minutes or until melted completely, stirring after every 30 seconds.
2. Remove from microwave and stir the mixture until smooth.
3. Add the sugar, and eggs and whisk until frothy.
4. Add the orange rind and juice, followed by flour and mix until well combined.
5. Divide mixture into 4 greased ramekins about ¾ full.
6. Arrange the "Crisper Basket" in the pot of Ninja Foodi Grill.
7. Close the Ninja Foodi Grill with lid and select "Air Crisp".
8. Set the temperature to 355 degrees F to preheat.
9. Press "Start/Stop" to begin preheating.
10. When the display shows "Add Food" open the lid and place the ramekins into the "Crisper Basket".
11. Close the Ninja Foodi Grill with lid and set the time for 12 minutes.
12. Press "Start/Stop" to begin cooking.
13. When the cooking time is completed, press "Start/Stop" to stop cooking and open the lid.
14. Place the ramekins set aside to cool completely before serving.

Nutritional Information per Serving:

Calories: 454 | Fat: 33.6g | Saturated Fat: 21.1g | Carbohydrates: 34.2g | Sugar: 28.4g | Protein: 5.7g

Printed in Great Britain
by Amazon